MAKE YOUR OWN MUSIC:
A Creative Curriculum Using
Music Technology

To access online media visit:
www.halleonard.com/mylibrary

Enter Code:

7823-2613-9528-5142

MAKE YOUR OWN MUSIC:
A Creative Curriculum Using Music Technology

MAKE YOUR OWN MUSIC:
A Creative Curriculum Using Music Technology

Richard McCready

Hal Leonard Books
An Imprint of Hal Leonard Corporation

Published in 2016 by Hal Leonard Books
An Imprint of Hal Leonard Corporation
7777 West Bluemound Road
Milwaukee, WI 53213

Trade Book Division Editorial Offices
33 Plymouth St., Montclair, NJ 07042

Printed in the United States of America

Book design by John J. Flannery

Library of Congress Cataloging-in-Publication Data
Names: McCready, Richard.
Title: Make your own music : a creative curriculum using music technology / Richard McCready.
Description: Montclair, NJ : Hal Leonard Books, 2016. | Includes bibliographical references.
Identifiers: LCCN 2015044343 | ISBN 9781480397453
Subjects: LCSH: Popular music--Instruction and study. | Popular music--Production and direction. | Studio One (Computer file) | Digital audio editors. | Notion (Computer file) | Musical notation--Computer programs.
Classification: LCC MT10 .M39 2016 | DDC 781.3/4--dc23
LC record available at http://lccn.loc.gov/2015044343

www.halleonardbooks.com

CONTENTS

Introduction ix
by John Mlynczak, M.M., M.Ed., Director of Educational Technology
for Noteflight LLC, a Hal Leonard company

Acknowledgments xiii

Chapter 1. Getting Started with Recording and Sequencing 1
Introduction...1
Skill One: Recording Using the Microphone.....................................6
Skill Two: Sequencing with Musicloops 10
Bonus Skill: Creating Fades 14
STEAM Problem Solving: How a Computer Hears Sound 15
Project A: Introducing Your Own Radio Show 18

Chapter 2. Getting Started with Music Notation 21
Introduction 21
Skill Three: Entering Notation in Notion 23
Skill Four: Creating a Simple Arrangement 29
Bonus Skill: Adding Swing 32
STEAM Problem Solving: How to Hear Things in 3D—
    The Panorama Effect 33
Project B: Creating an Arrangement of a Tune from
    John Playford's *The Dancing Master*...35

Chapter 3. Making Beats with Impact in Studio One....................39
Introduction..39
Skill Five: Creating a Drum Beat 40
Skill Six: Mixing Drums...45
Bonus Skill: Creating Musicloops...50
STEAM Problem Solving: Latency and How to Control It 50
Project C: Composing Music with Beats 53

Chapter 4. Using Chords in Notion 55
  Introduction..55
  Skill Seven: Composing a Piece of Music with
    a Repeating Chord Sequence 57
  Skill Eight: Preparing Your Score for Performance........................61
  Bonus Skill: Exporting Your Song from Notion.............................64
  STEAM Problem Solving: Producing Large Quantities of
    Sheet Music..65
  Project D: Composing Music with a Repeating Chord Sequence....67

**Chapter 5. Creating Electronic Music with
Virtual Instruments in Studio One** 69
  Introduction..69
  Skill Nine: Working with Mojito...70
  Skill Ten: Layering Soft Synths to Create
    a Binary-Form Composition 78
  Bonus Skill: Transposing..83
  STEAM Problem Solving: Creating Sound with Electronics............83
  Project E: Composing Electronic Music in Ternary Form 87

Chapter 6. Recording and Editing in Studio One 89
  Introduction..89
  Skill Eleven: Recording Vocals, Electric Guitars, Basses,
    and Other Instruments..89
  Skill Twelve: Composing Video Game Music by Layering Motifs...95
  Bonus Skill: Exporting from Studio One 98
  STEAM Problem Solving: Recording and Overdubbing 99
  Project F: Composing Music for Your Own Video Game..............103

Chapter 7. Mixing and Mastering in Studio One 105
  Introduction..105
  Skill Thirteen: Adding Plug-in Effects and Automation...............105
  Skill Fourteen: Final Mixing and Mastering 110
  Bonus Skill: Using Buses and Sends in Studio One.......................113
  STEAM Problem Solving: The Mixing Desk...................................114
  Project G: The Final Presentation 117

Chapter 8. Notes and Resources for Teachers 121
  The Creative Process and Assessment: Author's Perspective.........121
  Recommended Examples of Electronic Music for Listening 123
  Recommended Examples of Video Game Music 124

Reproducible Project Sheet: Project A 125
Reproducible Project Sheet: Project B 126
Reproducible Project Sheet: Project C 127
Reproducible Project Sheet: Project D 128
Reproducible Project Sheet: Project E 129
Reproducible Project Sheet: Project F 130
Reproducible Project Sheet: Project G 131

Index..133

INTRODUCTION

by John Mlynczak, M.M., M.Ed.
Director of Educational Technology
Noteflight LLC, a Hal Leonard Company

INTRODUCTION TO A CREATIVE CURRICULUM

> Creativity is just connecting things. When you ask creative people how they did something, they feel a little guilty because they didn't really do it, they just saw something. It seemed obvious to them after a while.
> —*Steve Jobs (1955–2011)*

To create, we just begin by connecting things around us and, eventually, the process becomes intuitive. Steve Jobs is absolutely correct here. Creativity is a skill we all need to be successful, both in music and in life. To create music freely, we must first understand the process and eliminate any barriers.

The National Core Arts Standards (NCAS) define four Artistic Processes: Creating, Performing, Responding, and Connecting. These are obviously sequential, because without the creation of content, there is nothing to perform, respond to, or connect to our world. This focus on creating in education goes beyond NCAS and is a driving force in Common Core State Standards, Project-based Learning, the Partnership for 21st Century Skills, and STEAM. (For details on these and other education standards, visit http://musiced.presonus. com/standards.)

For many of us, creativity feels out of our comfort zone. Unlike rehearsing and performing a piece of music, creativity requires an experimental and process-focused mindset. In some cases, our misperceptions of creativity hinder our ability to create effectively. This introduction explores and debunks five common myths about creativity:

Myth #1: Creativity means making up brand new ideas.

This is a common misconception both with composition and with musical improvisation. Improvisation is simply an instantaneous form of composition. Ask any great jazz player; they will tell you that improvising is certainly not making up new ideas on the spot, but drawing upon a vast library of rehearsed licks and motifs in various keys and modulations to create music in the moment.

The lessons in this book are a great introduction to creating because they provide content and allow time to try ideas, listen back, and refine your music. You do not need to make up anything new, and Studio One provides libraries of loops, sounds, and samples to help you get started. This is the ideal way to begin "connecting things" and making your own music.

Myth #2: Creativity means composing an entire piece of music.

Creativity is a process, not a product. A lesson on creativity does not necessarily have to end with a fully composed piece of music. Experimenting with an eight-measure loop is enough to provide hours of creative potential. These lessons focus on the process of creating, allowing you to enjoy making music.

Myth #3: We must have a clear outline before starting a project.

Creativity is messy, and messy is fun! Think of this text as a framework or a "sandbox" for creativity. Having too many tools and options can be overwhelming, but these lessons provide parameters and guidelines to structure your sandbox. Some lessons may include only a cup and some water, while others may include a shovel and that cool castle mold. The most important aspect is that, once the lesson structures the size of your sandbox and the tools you can use, feel free to explore, create, knock down, and start over; make a mess until you are proud of what you have created.

Myth #4: We must be able to read music and understand music theory to get started.

Music is a language, and language is first learned orally. Ask a six-year-old to tell you a story and listen to the child's imagination soar. Then, ask the same six-year-old to write you a story using only the words she can write and spell—major difference. Children will eventually learn to write and spell all the words in their oral stories, but their imagination will always lead the way, and so should ours.

Starting out with Studio One and making music with sounds allows you to make music right away. Over the course of the lessons provided, you will begin to understand how to write and "spell" all the sounds you are creating, and then begin to notate in Notion.

Myth #5: My music has to be perfect or it will get a bad grade.

The purpose of assessment is to help you improve, especially on the creative process. The rubrics and assessments included in Chapter Eight of this book are used to provide feedback on the process of making music in order to allow you to create to your potential. This way, you are free to make music and create while gaining valuable guidance.

Technology has changed the way we teach and learn music because it has changed the way we consume music. Luckily, it has never been easier to create music using computers, software, and hardware. The tools and lessons in this book allow you to connect things, enjoy the process of creating, play in the sand, tell your story, and interact with peers to get better at creating. So, it's time to get started making our own music!

ACKNOWLEDGMENTS

Many thanks to my parents, Sam and Joan McCready, for raising me to value the integrity of my art and for showing me how to teach.

Thanks also to my wife, Julia, for our shared love of fun, experiential, hands-on music learning, and to "the kids" Alice, George, and Margo.

Thanks to electronic music geniuses Chris Fyhr, Will Kuhn, and V. J. Manzo for their help in selecting and narrowing down the huge lists of recommended listening examples.

Thanks always to the members of TI:ME (Technology Institute for Music Educators) for continuing to spread the message of technology-based music learning for all students.

Thanks especially to John Mlynczak of Noteflight and Bill Gibson of Hal Leonard for their help with making this book happen.

MAKE YOUR OWN MUSIC:
A Creative Curriculum Using Music Technology

GETTING STARTED WITH RECORDING AND SEQUENCING

1

CHAPTER ONE GOAL AND OBJECTIVES

The goal of this chapter is to get you up and running with the PreSonus *Music Creation Suite* and Studio One DAW software. As you read and work through the chapter, you will

- Connect all parts of the PreSonus *Music Creation Suite* to your computer.
- Install Studio One and Notion.
- Record your voice using the PreSonus M7 microphone.
- Compose a short piece of music by sequencing, using Musicloops. *Sequencing* is a term we use to describe the process of placing short musical fragments together to create a composition.
- Create volume fades using automation lanes.
- Record an intro for a radio program.
- Understand and appreciate the technological contributions of David Edward Hughes, the inventor of the microphone.

INTRODUCTION

Music is a shared art. People compose and perform music because they want others to listen to it, maybe to understand their feelings, their emotions, or the stories of their lives. Maybe they want to create new sounds and harmonies that have never been heard before. Maybe they want to keep alive the music of their culture and heritage by continuing to write and perform this music. Whatever the motivation for creating music, it is an essential and enjoyable part of the human experience, which brings us to you and the reason you picked up this book.

This is a book about making music—about making your own music. Perhaps you've always wanted to compose your own music and write it down or record it for others to enjoy. It's fun to create your own music and hear it performed. Many people throughout the history of music have done exactly this. We know what music must have sounded like many hundreds of years ago because people wrote it down in some form of notation. *Notation* is just a fancy word for the type of written code that we associate with music reading: clefs, quarter notes, eighth notes, time signatures, key signatures, and so on. We know what Bach's music sounded like, what Beethoven's music sounded like, and what Mozart's music sounded like because they wrote it down (or sometimes somebody wrote it down for them) and we are able to play the notes from the written notation. By learning to read music, we can play exactly what people composed many years ago. We also know what music sounded like within the last century because of recording. Though important musicians such as Robert Johnson, John Lennon, Hank Williams, and Jimi Hendrix are no longer with us, we know exactly what their music sounded like because we are able to listen to it from the recordings they made when they were alive.

You have chosen to begin learning how to make your own music. By reading this book, practicing the skills, and completing the projects inside, you will learn how to compose music, how to write it into the computer using notation software, and how to record it and sequence it using Digital Audio Workstation software. Every skill covered in the following chapters has an accompanying tutorial available in the book's online companion.

Advances in computers and music-making software in the last years have allowed contemporary musicians to compose with an ease and quality that is inspirational. To compose music in our modern technological age, there are a number of requirements:

A computer. It doesn't matter if it's a Mac or a PC, so long as it passes the minimum requirements of the software you are going to run on it.

An audio interface. This is vital for recording because it converts between analog sound (the type you hear) and digital data (the type the computer understands).

A microphone. A good microphone is essential. The microphone that is included in your computer may be good enough for videoconferencing, but it's certainly not up to the task of recording music. You should not record acoustic instruments or voice with the computer's microphone, much as you would not shoot a movie with your computer's webcam, because it will be of very poor quality.

Headphones or speakers. To hear all the subtleties of the music you are writing and/or recording, you need a good pair of headphones or speakers (studio monitors). Again, even though your computer has built-in speakers, these are not generally up to the task of quality music recording and listening.

Notation software. You need a program to let you input notes and rhythms in notated format and to hear it played back with authentic sounds.

Digital Audio Workstation (also known as DAW) software. This type of program allows you to record into the computer, to program and edit MIDI data, to mix all the music together, and to render a final mastered version of your music for others to listen to.

MIDI Controller. This is the easiest way to input notes into the computer, whether you're recording, inputting MIDI data into DAW software, or entering notes into a notation program.

Cables. You need all the necessary wires to make the connections between your computer, audio interface, microphone, keyboard, and headphones/speakers.

A good pair of ears. No amount of expensive equipment can take the place of good listening skills when you are composing and creating your own music. Look after your hearing. Do not listen to loud music for long periods of time, do take frequent breaks to avoid fatigue when listening, and always make sure you are doing your work in a quiet area away from distractions.

I'm sure you can imagine that getting all of those items together requires quite a lot of research, shopping, patience, and cash. How do you know which is the best audio interface for your needs? How do you know what Digital Audio Workstation software to buy? How do you know what notation software is best for your level of expertise? There is also the question of whether your chosen keyboard audio interface will work with the software you use (for example, an audio interface might only work with 16-bit or 32-bit software, and you might have purchased a 64-bit DAW).

The *Music Creation Suite* by PreSonus has taken all those questions and narrowed them down to just one: what computer to use. When you buy the *Music Creation Suite*, you get a condenser microphone with case and stand, a 49-note MIDI Controller, a 2-input audio interface, a pair of headphones, microphone cable, USB cables, USB powered hub, Studio One DAW software, and Notion notation software, all for just $400 at the time of publication of this book. When you unpack the box and connect everything to your computer, it all works immediately. There's no need to reinstall drivers or operating systems nor make your way through complicated Control Panel settings or Audio/MIDI Setup screens. Just make sure your computer meets the requirements listed on the side of the *Music Creation Suite* box, and you should be good to go. When everything is connected, it should look something like this.

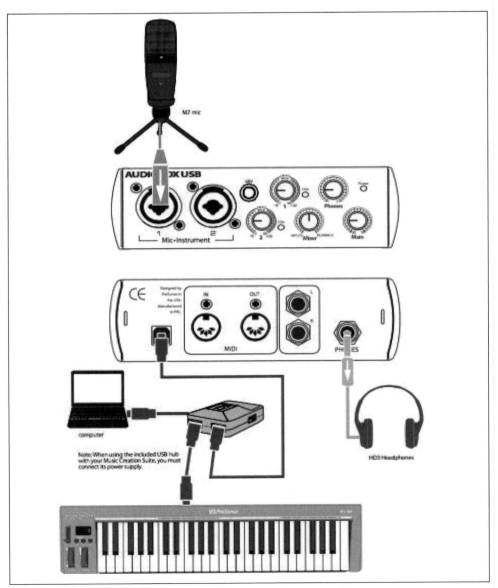

Figure 1-1. Music Creation Suite components connected to a computer.

Because the PreSonus *Music Creation Suite* has made everything so easy, this book uses the contents of the box as your equipment for learning to make your own music. After all, you want to be able to start making music quickly, not spend time dealing with annoying computer issues. This does not mean that you absolutely must have the PreSonus *Music Creation Suite* to use this book. If you already have Studio One, Notion, and a good audio interface, microphone, and headphones, you will certainly be able to enjoy learning the skills and completing the projects in the book.

Of course, you'll have to spend some time installing all the software and connecting your peripherals, but after you've done it once, you don't need to do it again. The *Music Creation Suite* comes with an installation guide, so work your way through it and make sure you have installed Studio One plus all the additional content, and Notion with all the extra sounds. If you have any difficulties, you can always contact PreSonus for support through your http:// my.presonus.com page or by calling PreSonus at 1-225-216-7887.

Throughout this book, you will find skills to learn and projects that build on these skills. Completing the projects will enable you to develop and practice your skills. The skills are each accompanied by an explanatory video in the book's online companion. These videos are an essential part of the process, and you should definitely watch them and use them in your learning. You will find them very helpful as they provide you with an alternative way of processing the information contained in the book.

In the book, you will also be able to read about STEAM Problem Solving. STEM is a very popular buzzword in education right now— it refers to applications in Science, Technology, Engineering, and Math, particularly with regard to creative problem solving. STEAM includes Arts in that mix, and a subject like Music Technology is a great example of how the Arts belong in the acronym—STEM becomes STEAM. In the STEAM Problem Solving sections throughout this book, you will see how inventors, musicians, composers, and producers used Science, Technology, Engineering, Arts, and Math together to make our modern world of Music Technology possible.

SKILL ONE: RECORDING USING THE MICROPHONE

1. Open Studio One and click on Create a new Song. From the Interfaces tab, select Audiobox USB, and also enter a name for your song. The actual name doesn't really matter—put some random words together or maybe just call it Skill One. Click OK.

2. You will see two tracks, both of which are armed for recording. One is labeled **Input L** and the other is labeled **Input R**. These obviously refer to the two inputs on your audio interface, marked 1 and 2. Disarm Track 2 (Input R) by clicking on the red record button in the track header. You can also delete the track if you want by selecting it and then choosing Remove Track from the Track menu (Track > Remove Track).

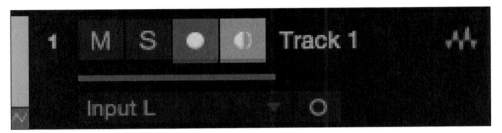

Figure 1-2. Studio One Track Header.

3. You need to turn on power to your microphone from the audio interface. The PreSonus *Music Creation Suite* comes with a type of microphone known as a *condenser microphone*. Condenser microphones need to have power supplied to them in order to work, and this is usually done from an audio interface (or a mixing board) via a switch labeled **48V**, **+48V**, or **Phantom Power**. Make sure your microphone is connected to Input 1 on your interface, and then turn on the 48V power. The 48V power switch on the PreSonus Audiobox USB glows red when it is engaged—a really neat feature.

   It is always best for your microphone if it is already connected before you turn the power on, and that you turn the power off before you disconnect the microphone. Note: you do not need to use 48V power if you are using a dynamic microphone or a ribbon microphone. If you are not sure what type of microphone you have, try recording without using 48V power first. If a signal shows up in Studio One as you test the microphone, then your microphone isn't a condenser, so please don't shock it by suddenly turning the 48V power on. If turning on the power to the microphone creates a signal where there wasn't one before, then your microphone is more than likely a condenser mic.

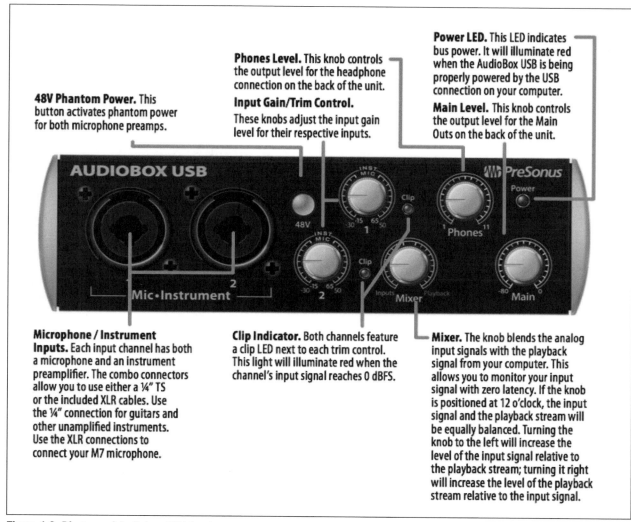

Figure 1-3. Diagram of Audiobox USB front.

4. Make sure your headphones are connected, and then turn the Phones dial on the Audiobox USB to about 9 o'clock. Turn the Mixer dial left all the way to Inputs. Find the Gain dial for channel 1 on your audio interface (on the Audiobox USB, it is right beside the 48V button) and turn it all the way left. Now, with the microphone about 3 to 6 inches from your mouth, start speaking. Turn the Gain dial to the right while you speak, and you will start to see the signal bar in the Track 1 track header fill up with

signal. As you keep speaking, keep turning the Gain dial right until the orange clip light comes on. Then turn the dial back a couple of clicks so the clip light goes out. If everything is good, you should see a very strong signal coming into Studio One with no clip light. If the sound you hear in your headphones is too loud or too quiet, adjust the Phones dial.

If you do not like hearing your own voice as you record, turn the Mixer dial away from Inputs toward 12 o'clock or turn off the blue Monitoring button in the track header. It is important that you leave the Gain dial right where you set it when you found a strong input signal level for your voice.

5. Find the transport section of Studio One (Figure 1-4). Click on the Record button (it looks like a circle on a square and lights up red when you click it). Begin speaking into the microphone. Maybe read a poem, recite the alphabet, read a favorite passage from a book (it could even be this book), or just say something completely random. You don't need to start speaking as soon as you hit Record—you can edit out the pre-roll later. As you record, you should see a waveform start to draw in Track 1— this is known as an *audio event*. When you're finished recording, click the Stop button in the transport (it looks like a square on a square and turns blue-green when you click it).

Figure 1-4. The transport in Studio One.

6. If you messed up, you can always redo your recording. Click cmd-Z (ctrl-Z on a PC) to undo your recording, click the Return-to-Zero button (to the left of the Stop button) to return the transport to the start of the song, and record again.

7. Save your work. Really. It's a good idea to get into a habit of saving your work every time you finish recording or editing something. Sudden power surges or accidental loss of power to your computer can sometimes undo a lot of really good work, so remember to save as often as reasonably possible. You can select Save from the File menu (File > Save) or use the shortcut key combination cmd-S (ctrl-S on a PC).

8. If you hover the mouse over the left or right end of the audio region you just created in Track 1, you will see the cursor change to a line and an arrow. By holding down the mouse button, you can trim the front and back end of the region to delete the pre-roll and post-roll from your recording. *Pre-roll* and *post-roll* are terms from the old days of tape machines, when extra reel-to-reel or cassette tape rolled before and after the recording, but we still use those expressions even though nothing actually rolls across your desk while you record.

9. Try hovering over the top of the region, halfway between the start and end of the recording. A small square will appear. Click and drag that square either up or down and you will see the shape of the recorded waveform change. As the waveform gets larger, it gets louder, and as it gets smaller, it gets softer. This is a very quick way to alter the level of a recording, though it should not be used to make up for inefficiently setting the recording levels.

10. Now hover over another part of the region (the cursor will become an arrow) and drag the audio event to the start of the song. Turn your audio interface's Mixer dial all the way right to Playback and you'll be able to listen to your recording using the transport on Studio One. If you double-click on the region, you'll be able to see what the waveform looks like in the Edit view. We'll learn more about this view later in the book. When you are happy with what you hear, save your work.

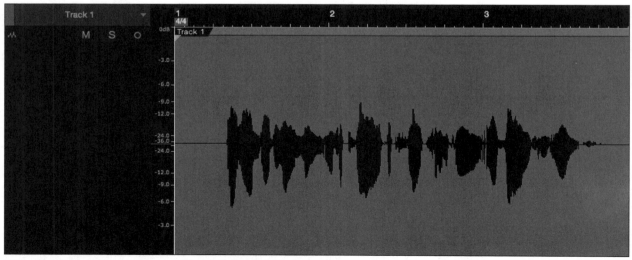

Figure 1-5. Recorded waveform event in Studio One's Edit view.

That's it—your first skill. It may seem very simple just to record one track of spoken voice and listen back to it, but it's essential that you learn early on to record good sound. If your input signal is weak you will pick up a lot of noise as you turn the volume up for playback, and you don't want that. If your input signal is too strong, you will introduce a nasty metallic sound known as *digital distortion*, and you don't want that either. Knowing how to place a microphone correctly relative to the sound source and to set a good recording level are non-negotiable basic skills in Music Technology. Learning to do it correctly at a beginning stage saves many headaches later on.

SKILL TWO: SEQUENCING WITH MUSICLOOPS

1. Create a new song in Studio One, either from the Start page or by selecting File > New Song. Choose the Empty Song template and give your song a name. Again, the name does not really matter at

Figure 1-6. Creating a new song in Studio One.

this stage, so just think of something random. Before you click OK, make sure that the box beside Stretch audio files to Song tempo is checked and that the box beside Timebase is set to Bars.

2. On the Audio Setup screen, which you will find by selecting Preferences from the Studio One menu (Studio One > Preferences > Audio Setup), make sure that the Audiobox USB is selected as your Audio Device and then confirm by clicking OK.

3. If it is not already in view to the right of the Arrange view, open the Studio One browser by clicking on the Browse button at the bottom right of the screen. Choose the tab marked Loops, and you will find a series of folders that are installed on your machine. If the folders are not there, make sure you go to Studio One > Studio One Installation and install all the packets available for you from your PreSonus user account.

4. Beneath the Loops tab are three more tabs that allow you to choose to sort the loops by various methods. As you get used to the library of Musicloops, you will be able to set these to sort this library so you can easily find your favorite loops. You will also see a magnifying-glass icon at the top right of the browser. Click this and then type a search term (maybe a favorite instrument or genre, such as "guitar" or "rock") and hit Enter. As you type the search terms, you will see that Studio One finds items in the library that match those terms. The browser contains two types of files—.wav files and Musicloops, as you can see by the end of each file name. The .wav files are usually one-shot recordings (a drum hit, a chord, a single note), and the Musicloops are longer excerpts of music. An important difference between them is that the Musicloops will stretch to match the project tempo, while the .wav files will not. You will need to use just the Musicloop type for this composition skill.

5. Select one of the Musicloops that Studio One found by clicking on it. If you have too many to choose from, enter another search term to narrow the focus of the search. As you click a Musicloop, a small window opens underneath the browser that gives you more information about the Musicloop you selected. You can listen to it by clicking the Play triangle underneath the word Musicloop. The Stop button will stop the playback. Make sure you have a good volume to your headphones from your Audiobox USB audio interface, and check that the Mixer dial is at Playback.

6. The button next to the Stop button is a Loop button that allows you to continue listening to the loop several times, until you hit Stop, and the fourth button is a Metronome button that turns on a click so you can hear how the loop sounds against the tempo of the song. As a loop is playing, you can adjust the song tempo by clicking on the tempo in the transport and dragging up or down, or by clicking and then entering a new tempo manually using the numbers on your computer keyboard. Tempo (or speed) is measured in *bpm*—that stands for *beats per minute*.

Figure 1-7. The Musicloop Preview Window.

7. When you find a Musicloop you like, drag it from the browser into the Arrange view (this is the part of Studio One where your tracks are located). As you drag the Musicloop over, you will see a preview of it. Drag the Musicloop to the position you want it (probably the beginning of the song) and drop it. You will see a new track created with the same name as the Musicloop you dragged over. You can change this name to something simpler just by double-clicking on the name of the new track and typing something else.

8. When you drag a Musicloop into a new track, you will notice that it looks different from the audio event you worked with in Skill One (Figure 1-5), resembling more a set of broken horizontal lines. This is because Musicloops do not actually contain sound—they simply show you the data that tells the computer what notes to play. Double-click on the event to see it in the Edit view. Here, you can see the notes laid out in something we call Piano-roll view, and you'll see how the Edit view contains a lot of ways you can edit the data. If you move some of the notes around, the pitches change. If you do this with the data in a drum loop, the drum sounds change! Try experimenting with adding different loops into the Arrange view and altering the data in the Edit view.

To close the Edit view again, simply click the Edit button in the bottom right of Studio One. Interestingly, if you drag a Musicloop over a previously created audio track (like the ones you made in Skill One), Studio One will render the Musicloop as an audio event and show you the audio waveform view with the original data layered on top.

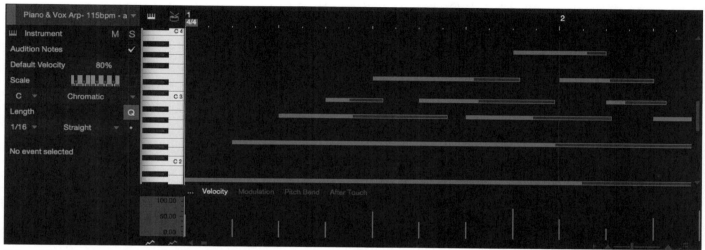

Figure 1-8. Instrument data event in Studio One's Edit view.

9. To repeat a Musicloop in the Arrange view, select it and press the letter D on your computer keyboard. You can also move a Musicloop left or right by dragging it with your mouse, or copy it by holding the option key (Alt key on a PC) while you drag. Note that any changes you have made in the Musicloop are kept as you move or copy the Musicloop. Also note that all loops in your song conform to the song tempo.

10. Try adding different Musicloops to your song. Remove the search terms in the browser by clicking on the X at the end of each search term, and then try new search terms. If you don't like something after you drag it to the Arrange view, just delete the track (Track > Remove Track). As you create more tracks, you will notice that they are all represented in different shades of gray-blue, and it begins to get a bit dull color-wise. Click on the color bar at the far left of a track to change its color.

11. Open the Mix view by clicking on the Mix button at the bottom right of Studio One. Now you will notice your tracks lined up horizontally rather than vertically. If you color-coded your tracks and gave them simpler names, you'll see how this is du-

plicated in the Mix view. Here, you can alter the balance of the instruments in your song by moving the faders up and down. Above the faders, you will also notice horizontal sliders for panning. This allows you to move the sounds in your song more toward one side of your headphones or the other. Ideally, you want to imagine how your instruments would line up on a stage and then use the panning sliders to place them. Don't go overboard and pan things too far to the left or right. Hard panning is really just for effects. In good mixing, you want to keep your instruments within 30 to 45 degrees to each side of center or things start sounding quite artificial.

12. To the right of the Mix view, you will see the fader for the Main Out bus of Studio One (a *bus* is a channel that contains many tracks of sound mixed together). As you add more sounds into your song, you may see the top of the volume meter go red. This is called *clipping*, and it creates digital distortion in your sound. Try to keep your faders at conservative levels so that this does not happen. If the song is too quiet for your ears, you should turn up your headphone level on your Audiobox USB audio interface and not push the faders until Studio One distorts. We will learn later in the book about other ways to control volume and distortion, but for now, good practice is always to keep an eye on that volume level and use your Mix view faders accordingly.

13. Every time you create something cool, save your work. You're probably beginning to work quite quickly now with adding and editing Musicloops, and it would be a shame to lose your song if the computer suddenly froze (although Studio One very rarely freezes) or you lost power.

BONUS SKILL: CREATING FADES

1. Open the song you created in Skill Two.
2. Make sure you can see your Mix view.
3. Ctrl-click (right-click on a PC) on one of the faders and select Edit Volume Automation. Studio One will draw an extra track in the Arrange view, underneath the track you selected.

Figure 1-9. Volume Automation Track.

4. As you mouse over the vertical line in this new track, the cursor becomes a finger. Click on the line to create breakpoints—they look like tiny circles. You can now click and drag any breakpoint up to raise the volume or down to lower the volume at that breakpoint.

5. Place a breakpoint near the end of the song where you want a fade-out to start. Place another breakpoint right at the end of the song and drag it all the way down. Now, as you listen back to your song, you will see the volume fader lower itself all the way down as the track fades out.

At this point, you have learned two important skills: recording using a microphone and working with Musicloops, as well as the bonus skill of creating fades. You are ready to tackle Project A: Introducing Your Own Radio Show.

Feel free to pause here and spend some time really practicing these skills. Record things other than your voice (maybe an acoustic guitar, piano, or clarinet) and make several songs by combining Musicloops. Perhaps you could even create a song with Musicloops, add an audio track (Track > Add Audio Track [mono]), and sing or rap over your song. The important ideas are to get used to moving things around in the Arrange view; learn how to get a good strong signal from your microphone; learn how to navigate the transport; learn how to get to the Browse, Edit, and Mix views; and have fun. You'll know when it's time to move to the next chapter, in which you'll start checking out the notation editor, Notion.

STEAM PROBLEM SOLVING: HOW A COMPUTER HEARS SOUND

The process of getting sound into and out of the computer is actually quite simple and is totally dependent on the science of sound, which we call *acoustics*. Sound is made up of different speeds of vibrating air. Your ears are capable of feeling the vibrations in the air and telling your brain what you are hearing. The computer doesn't have ears, so it needs some help understanding what sound is.

Here's how it works: Your microphone is a delicate device that is able to feel the vibration of air and convert it to an electrical voltage. That voltage is then converted to digital data by the Audiobox USB interface and is represented in Studio One as a waveform

(Figure 1-5). As you play back the waveform from Studio One, the audio interface converts the digital data back to voltage. When this voltage is sent through speakers or headphones (which are actually just a very small pair of speakers that you wear on your head), the voltage is converted back to air vibrations that your ears then pass to your brain as sound. The audio interface is the essential link, and so a good quality audio interface such as the PreSonus Audiobox USB is critical to good recording.

The microphone is an example of a type of device we call a *transducer*—it takes one form of energy (sound waves) and converts it to another (voltage). A speaker is also a transducer, but it converts voltage to sound waves. Headphones contain tiny speakers, known as *drivers*, in each earpiece. In a simple way, a speaker is a backward microphone.

There is no doubt that we would have no such thing as recording without the invention of the microphone, which is generally credited to a Welsh physicist and musician named David Edward Hughes (1831–1900). Though he was born in Wales, in the United Kingdom, his family immigrated to the United States when Hughes was just seven years old. He was quite a prodigy, learning to play the harp by the age of six, and subsequently becoming a virtuoso pianist. He later became a professor of music at St Joseph's College in Bardstown, Kentucky.

Hughes loved to tinker with electricity, and he created a number of telegraph and telephone-type devices. He invented the microphone in the mid-1870s as a device for converting the air vibrations created by the human voice into an electrical signal so that a human could be heard distinctly in a telephone conversation. His *carbon microphone* (as it was called) was essentially a transducer that changed sound to voltage.

When Hughes invented his device, he decided not to patent it. He wanted to give it to the world as a gift because he realized the enormous potential it would have in telephony. He probably had no clue that it would become so widely used in music and broadcasting today.

Emile Berliner and Thomas Edison both also created a type of carbon microphone quite independently, and both filed for the patent in 1877. There was a legal battle, and Thomas Edison was

Figure 1-10. David Edward Hughes.

granted the patent, though he was not actually the first to come up with the technology.

All microphones use a capsule to convert sound waves to voltage. The type of capsule determines whether the microphone is dynamic, condenser, ribbon, or some other type. A condenser microphone, like the PreSonus M7 that is included in the *Music Creation Suite*, operates via a small diaphragm that feels the vibration of air coming in and moves accordingly. The distance between the diaphragm and a static plate is then measured and transmitted by the microphone as voltage. The tiny amount of movement required to create the electrical signal means that condenser microphones are very precise in their recording quality, but are not capable of handling large sound pressure levels (very loud noises). They are somewhat fragile and should be handled carefully. Dust and dirt can render a condenser microphone less precise, so you should keep your microphone protected in its case whenever you are not using it.

PROJECT A: INTRODUCING YOUR OWN RADIO SHOW

In this project, you use the skills you learned in Chapter One to record an introduction to a radio show, with yourself as host. Create some intro music by combining and altering Musicloops, record yourself introducing the show, and finish with some outro music, again using Musicloops. Your entire project should last less than one minute.

When you record your voice, you need to make sure you get a strong signal and introduce yourself with your own name (or a nickname), the title of your show, and the name of your radio station.

You should have a minimum of five tracks in your project, and you should use different search terms to find each Musicloop that you use. Your intro and outro music should ideally reflect the type of music that you want listeners to enjoy on your radio show.

HELPFUL TIPS

- Record your voice first. Your introduction of yourself should be proud and confident. You should think carefully about the best way to introduce yourself and your show and probably rehearse a few times before you hit the Record button. Maybe you could say something like "Hello everybody out there in Radio Land! This is Johnny Smith welcoming you to the New Techno Music Show here on radio station WXYZ in New York City."
- If you stumble and need to record again, you can always press cmd-Z (ctrl-Z on a PC) to undo a recording and start over. Try not to speak too fast when you record—take your time.

- When you work on adding your Musicloops, you can mute your voice track by clicking on the M button underneath the title of your track. Don't forget to unmute it later.
- You can move your recorded voice event into position by dragging it left or right in the track.
- You can copy any event by pressing D on your computer keyboard, or you can hold the option key (alt on a PC) as you drag the event over.
- Remember that the Mixer dial on the front of the Audiobox USB switches between what you are recording (Inputs) and what the computer is playing back to you (Playback).
- Color-code and name your tracks as you record them or create them using Musicloops.

PROJECT REQUIREMENTS CHECKLIST

Your project should include

- Your own voice introducing your radio show, recorded well.
- Intro music using Musicloops.
- Outro music using Musicloops.
- A minimum of five tracks.
- At least five Musicloops, chosen by using different search terms.
- No more than one minute of total project length.
- Color-coded and properly titled tracks.
- A written summary of your challenges and successes in completing this project.

GETTING STARTED WITH MUSIC NOTATION

2

CHAPTER TWO GOAL AND OBJECTIVES

The goal of this chapter is to get you started using Notion by transcribing and arranging music from *The Dancing Master,* by John Playford. As you read and work through the chapter, you will

- Enter notes and rests in Notion using the mouse.
- Enter notes in Notion using the PS-49 MIDI Controller.
- Transcribe a tune from *The Dancing Master,* by John Playford.
- Arrange the tune for an ensemble by adding other instruments.
- Add swing to notes.
- Create your own arrangement of a tune from John Playford's *The Dancing Master.*
- Pan sounds left and right in a mix.

INTRODUCTION

The ability to read and write standard music notation is a very valuable skill for any musician. For many years, notation was the most efficient way for a composer to preserve his or her music for someone else to play. A lot of great music was written before recording was invented, so the only way we know how to perform this music is because the composers wrote it down in notation.

There are many different types of notation. Guitar players may use tablature that shows where to play notes on the instrument, jazz players may use lead sheets that contain melody and chords only, country players may use Nashville numbers in which a song is written out according to the relative numbers of each chord in a scale, and members of a contemporary music ensemble may use music that more resembles a graph or spreadsheet than anything we might interpret as music notes.

Standard notation, in which music is represented on a system of five-line staves, dates from around the 16th century, and there are many earlier versions of similar systems using different numbers of lines, including forms of lute and organ tablature. The invention of the printing press in 1570 was hugely important for the reproduction of music, as composers found they could make steady income by having their music published in printed form and sold in music stores. The sale of sheet music was the major way in which music was distributed before recording was invented. Consequently, the ability to read and write music in standard notation became critical for anybody who wanted to make music.

The age of the computer has made it less critical to have music-reading and -writing skills using standard notation. Being able to record your own music has meant that other people can learn from the recording or from a YouTube video. Many successful musicians in the world today do not read or write music well, but they can use their skills of listening and musicianship to have successful musical careers. The ability to play an instrument and the ability to read music are actually different skills, though obviously one may help with the other. Ultimately, it's best to understand that reading and writing music notation are skills you can learn, and you will never regret having these abilities, even if just at a rudimentary level.

Notation may look complicated at first, but it is actually quite straightforward and logical once you get the hang of it. It is a form of code, in which notes are represented by symbols that indicate rhythm according to the type of symbol and pitch according to the symbol's placement on the staff. The system of measures, in which music is divided into equal groups of beats, and the system of keys, in which music is grouped into sets of notes adhering to a scale, actually make the system easier to read, though some study of music theory is necessary to speed up music-reading skills.

If you have never tried to read music, it is quite important that you spend some time getting comfortable with how the system works before you progress through this chapter. You can find many books about music reading at a bookstore or video tutorials on the Internet that can help you learn the basics. You should be familiar with what the different notes are and where you find them on the staff, what time signatures and key signatures are, and what the symbols are for whole notes, half notes, quarter notes, eighth notes, and sixteenth notes, and their equivalent rest symbols. I strongly recommend the book *Music Theory* by Barrett Tagliarino, published by Hal Leonard (a very quick read with included exercises to help you practice), the excellent series of video tutorials at http://www.daveconservatoire.org, or the "Music Theory for Musicians and Normal People" website at http://tobyrush.com/theory pages/index.html.

Notion is PreSonus's music notation writing program, and it comes with sound samples recorded by members of the London Symphony Orchestra. Using Notion, you'll be able to compose and write music for others to play, and you'll be able to export your compositions in either audio or MIDI format and then import these into Studio One. You can also buy Notion as an app for your iPad, allowing you to email or DropBox Notion compositions to yourself and work on them on your iOS device. You could even put your iPad on your music stand and play your compositions without having to print out the parts.

Notion allows you to enter music by a number of different methods. You can use the mouse to place notes on the staff and click them in, you can use the on-screen fretboard or piano keyboard views, you can play the notes individually from your MIDI Controller, or if you have piano skills, you can play the music in real time and Notion will transcribe it into music notation for you.

SKILL THREE: ENTERING NOTATION IN NOTION

Before you start, make sure your audio interface and MIDI Controller are connected to your computer. There is a power switch on the back of the PreSonus PS-49 MIDI Controller that should be turned to the on position. You will know that the MIDI Controller has power if you can see a number in the LCD display on the left side of the controller. The Mixer dial on the front of the Audiobox USB should be turned to Playback, and the Headphone dial should be at a comfortable level for you to listen.

When you first open Notion, you will be taken to the Startup page. Before progressing any further, you need to ensure Notion is sending sound to your audio interface. Select Preferences from the Notion menu (Notion > Preferences) and choose the Audio tab. Choose the appropriate audio interface from the audio devices box. Notion will remember your preferences, so you won't need to change this again (although if you accidentally start Notion without your audio interface connected, Notion will return to selecting the built-in output; if that happens, you'll know how to fix it).

We're going to practice entering notes into Notion by inputting a simple tune published by the English sheet music publisher John Playford in 1651 in a book called *The Dancing Master*. Playford himself was not much of a composer, but he collected dancing tunes from the London society of the day and wrote them down in his books so others could learn the tunes and the dance steps. When you stop to think about it for a moment, it is quite amazing that we can use a computer program to hear the tunes that John Playford published, considering that he wrote it down in music notation almost 400 years ago. We can then use the same computer program to create our own version, or arrangement, of that same tune. It's almost like having your own crazy musical time machine.

John Playford's music has been arranged for instrumental ensembles and recorded by many musicians, and a YouTube or Spotify search for his name will bring up many excellent recordings. If you can, try to listen to any tracks from two particularly excellent albums: *A Trip to Killburn* by The Baltimore Consort or *English Country Dances* by The Broadside Band.

The tune we are going to work with was given the title "Argeers" by John Playford, and here's what the notation looked like when it was published in his book in 1651. It's pretty difficult to read, but you can certainly see the system of five lines and the music symbols that make up the melody.

Figure 2-1. "Argeers" facsimile from *The Dancing Master* (John Playford, 1651).

Here's what it looks like when written out in Notion. It's a good bit easier to read and looks just like a printed piece of sheet music. This is definitely the version you should copy as you complete the steps to learn this skill.

Figure 2-2. "Argeers" written out in Notion.

1. Open Notion and choose the option for New Score from the Startup page, or if you already have Notion open, you can choose New from the File menu (File > New). You are now in the Score Setup screen. Click on Strings on the right side and select Violin (solo). Click on Exit Score Setup at the top of the screen.

2. Double-click Title at the top of the score and type in "Argeers," then double-click Composer and type "John Playford," and finally double-click Date and type "from 'the Dancing Master' (1651)." Hit Enter after typing each piece of text.

3. You now have a score with a staff for a violin that already has a treble clef and a time signature of 4/4. You do not need to change these. However, you will need to add a key signature for G major. You will see some tabs with music symbols on them at the bottom of the screen—this is the entry palette. As you click tabs in the entry palette, they open up into more detail. This is where you can find almost everything you need to use in Notion. Find the tab that looks like three sharps with a time signature, click on it, and then find the icon that also shows three sharps. Click on that and you will see the Key Signature dialog. Change the Tonic to G and click OK. You will now see that the cursor has become one sharp symbol (the correct key signature for G major). Click in the shaded area at the start of the first measure, and Notion puts it in the correct place for the key signature of G major.

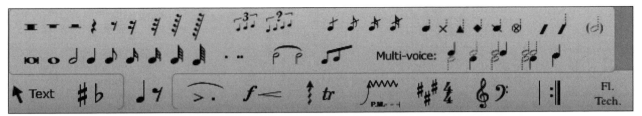

Figure 2-3. The entry palette in Notion.

Hit the Escape key on your keyboard and your cursor will return to normal. Notion works by loading musical symbols into the cursor so that you can place them into the score; you will find that you will be using the entry palette and Escape key a lot as you load and unload the cursor to change symbols or move around the score. It is a very efficient and simple way to work. You may find it easier to work in Notion if you zoom in on the score—hold the cmd key (ctrl on a PC) and press the equal sign (=) to zoom in or the minus sign (-) to zoom out.

4. Find the entry palette tab that looks like a quarter note followed by an eighth rest. This is where you will find all note and rest values. Click and then select an eighth note. The first note of "Argeers" is a G, so click on the G line in the staff; Notion draws a G for you. If you make a mistake, just press cmd-Z (ctrl-Z on a PC) to undo. The next three notes are A, B, C, so click those notes in. Notice that Notion adds the beams to the eighth notes.

   Now you need quarter notes, so change your cursor to a quarter note via the entry palette and enter the next four notes: A, G, F♯, D. You don't need to add a ♯ symbol for the F because it's already in the key signature. Now change the cursor to a half note and enter another D. As you go through the next measures, you will need a dot to make the dotted quarters in measure 3 and measure 6. After you click the quarter note in the entry palette, select the dot symbol just beside the smallest note symbol, and your cursor will become a dotted quarter. When you select an eighth for the next note, the dot will be dropped. Make your way through to the end of measure 8 and stop. Save your work by selecting Save from the File menu (File > Save).

5. At the end of measure 8, you need an "end repeat" sign. You will find this by selecting the entry palette tab that has a measure line and a repeat sign—you are looking for the symbol that has two vertical dots followed by two lines. When you place this

symbol into the score, make sure you place it at the end of measure 8. If you place it too far to the right, into measure 9, Notion will place it at the end of measure 9. Obviously you would need to press cmd-Z (ctrl-Z on a PC) to undo this and try again.

Listen to what you've done so far—find the transport at the top of the screen, click on the Rewind button (exactly the same as Return-to-Zero in Studio One), and then click on the Play button. You should now hear "Argeers" played by a violin. The program will return to the beginning after measure 8 and play the first eight measures a second time.

Figure 2-4. The transport in Notion.

6. Now we're going to try entering notes from the MIDI Controller. Hit Escape and click in the beginning of measure 9. Open the virtual keyboard by clicking the piano keyboard icon on the Toolbar at the top right of the screen, and you will see the on-screen virtual keyboard appear under the entry palette. To the left of the virtual keyboard are four buttons. The top two are melody mode and chord mode—make sure melody mode is selected. The bottom two buttons are edit mode and chord audition. Select edit mode (pencil icon), then choose an eighth note from the entry palette, and then press F♯4 followed by G4 on your MIDI Controller (or click F♯4 followed by G4 on the virtual keyboard). You will see that Notion enters these notes into measure 9. Now choose a quarter note from the entry palette and press A4. Keep going this way and you'll be able to enter the rest of the music up to measure 16. Notice that if you hit Escape at any time, you will need to select edit mode again.

Figure 2-5. The Toolbar in Notion.

Figure 2-6. The virtual keyboard.

7. When you've completed the music to measure 16, you'll need to delete the unused measures. Hit Escape to clear out your cursor, and then click and draw a box from above the top left of measure 17 down to beneath the bottom right of the last measure. When you release the mouse, you'll see that Notion has highlighted all the empty measures; you can now delete them by selecting Edit > Delete.

8. Double-check that you have entered all the correct notes and then listen to "Argeers" the whole way through. You can change the speed of the song by double-clicking the "quarter=60 bpm" marking at the start of the score and typing in a new number. In actual fact, "Argeers" would have been performed at quite a brisk tempo, so try changing the tempo to 160 or 180 beats per minute.

9. Save your work—you will be using this song for the next skill.

If you have piano-playing skills, you might like to try recording notes into Notion. Go ahead and create a new song and set it up for "Argeers" the same way you did in steps 1 through 3 of Skill Three. Click the Record button (red circle) in the transport and you will see the Recording Options dialog. Leave the options exactly as they are and click on Start Recording. After you hear four metronome clicks, play "Argeers" on your MIDI Controller straight through in time with the click. You'll be able to hear what you're playing through your headphones. There's no need to repeat the first eight measures—you can add the repeat sign once you're done. After you've played the song the whole way through, click on the Stop button on the transport, and Notion will magically fill the staff with the music you just played! If you played some wrong notes or your timing was inaccurate, you will see that reflected in your score, but you can always delete notes and re-enter them using the mouse, or you can undo everything and record again. Even if you have to take two or three tries at recording the whole song, it's probably faster in the long run than entering everything note by note using the entry palette.

Here's a neat trick: You can always slow down the metronome before you record by changing the bpm marker at the start of the song, and then speed it up again after you've recorded!

SKILL FOUR: CREATING A SIMPLE ARRANGEMENT

The music that John Playford wrote out in *The Dancing Master* was rarely played by a solo instrument, as individual musical instruments were far too quiet in those days for the music to be heard by the dancers or the audience. This was long before the days of amplifiers and microphones, of course, so the only way to make music louder was to add more instruments. When Playford first heard his tunes performed, he would have heard the melodies played together by many instruments, perhaps with some simple harmonies and some drums as well, so that's exactly what we are going to do next with "Argeers"—we're going to use Notion to help us transform it into an arrangement that would not have sounded completely out of place in the mid-17th century.

1. You will need to use your saved version of "Argeers," so select Open from the Startup page or select File > Open to open it.

2. The first thing we're going to do is add a couple of instruments to play the melody along with the solo violin. Open the Score Setup screen by clicking on the cog icon in the top right of the screen. Mouse over the Brass category and select a trumpet, and then mouse over the Woodwinds and select a flute. You should have three instruments now in your score. Click Exit Score Setup.

3. Of course, it would be a pain to have to enter all the notes again for the two new instruments, but Notion makes it easy. You'll notice that Notion has already put the correct key signature and time signature in the new trumpet and flute parts. Click in the first measure of the violin part (make sure you click somewhere other than a note head). Select Edit > Select Part and Notion will select the whole violin part. Select Edit > Copy (cmd-C on Mac or ctrl-C on a PC) and then click in the first measure of the trumpet part. Select Edit > Paste (cmd-V on Mac or ctrl-V on a PC) and Notion copies the entire part into the trumpet line. Now select the first measure in the flute part and select Edit > Paste again. Notice you did not have to reselect the violin part, because the notes were still copied to the computer's Clipboard.

4. Let's see what happens if we add an acoustic guitar part. Go to the Score Setup screen and add an acoustic guitar from the Guitars / Basses category. You'll notice that Notion gives you

two guitar staves in the score, one for notation and one for tab. Copy the violin part notes into the notation staff and you'll see that Notion automatically adds the tab for you. This is a very handy feature, especially if you don't know how to write tab yourself but you have a guitarist in the band who prefers to read tab. You will also notice that the notes in the guitar part are written an octave higher than you might think. This is because the guitar is actually a transposing instrument—it sounds an octave lower than the written pitch. Transpose the notes of the guitar part down an octave by pressing the down arrow on your computer keyboard seven times while the part is selected. You'll notice the tab works itself out as well as you move the notes. Once you've moved the guitar part down, it will sound an octave lower than the violin.

5. Now add an upright bass from the Guitars / Basses category. Even if you don't know the notes on the bass clef, it doesn't matter—Notion does the work for you. Copy the notes of the violin part into the new upright bass part. You'll see that the notes copy at pitch—very high in the bass clef. You will need to bring them down two octaves. You can do this by hitting the down arrow fourteen times, or you can use Notion's Transpose function (see Figure 2-7). With the part selected, choose Tools > Transpose, and you will see the Transpose dialog. Choose the options Perfect, Octave, Down, Chromatic, Two Octaves, and then click OK.

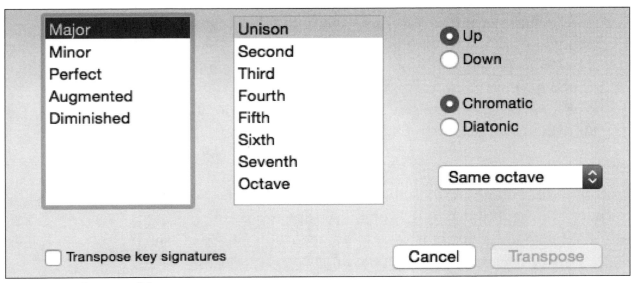

Figure 2-7. The Transpose dialog.

6. Now we'll add a simple harmony by having a viola play the melody a perfect fourth below the violin. This was a simple harmonic device that was used a lot in music of several hundred years ago and is used frequently in rock music today. Add a solo viola (Strings category) from the Score Setup screen. Viola players read in alto clef, but it doesn't matter whether you know how to read alto clef or not—Notion does. Copy the notes from the violin part into your viola part. Now select Tools > Transpose and transpose the viola part down by a perfect fourth—you will need to choose these options in the transpose dialog: Perfect, Fourth, Down, Chromatic, Same Octave.

7. Finally, let's add some drums. Drummers read drum notation that uses five lines of staff just like regular notation, but the type of drum hit is determined by the type of note head used (regular, cross, triangle, and so on), and the actual drum to be hit is determined by the vertical line or space on which the note head is placed. Again, you don't need to be proficient at drum notation to write a drum part because Notion includes a lot of sample drum rhythms and writes them out in drum notation for you. Add a drum set from the Drums / Cymbals category in the Score Setup screen. Click on the Drum Library icon to the right of the Virtual Keyboard icon. At the bottom of the screen, you will see eight virtual drum pads. Choose one of the styles to the right of the pads (Funk, Jazz, Rock, and World) and then click on one of the listed drum patterns in the rightmost box. As you move the cursor back over the score, you will see that the cursor is now the name of the pattern you chose. Click that into the first measure and Notion will draw the appropriate drum notation for that pattern. You can now click that same pattern into other measures, or choose a different pattern from the Drum Library. Of course, John Playford lived long before the days of drummers playing funk, jazz, rock, and World rhythms, but that doesn't matter—this is your arrangement.

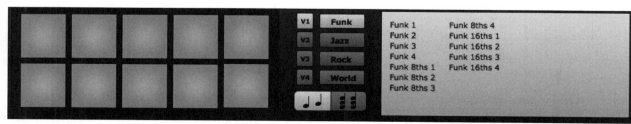

Figure 2-8. The Drum Library.

8. Hopefully, as you worked through these steps, you took some time to listen to your score as each new instrument was added. By the time you get this far, you'll probably notice that there are some balance issues—some instruments are louder than others, and some cannot be heard at all. You can fix this with Notion's Virtual Mixer, much as you would fix this problem in Studio One with the Mix view. To get to the Virtual Mixer, click on the Mixer icon to the right of the Score Setup icon. Now adjust the levels of each instrument using the faders, and separate them out using the panorama controls above the fader. Notice how you can move the sound left or right and also control the width of the sound in the panorama field by adjusting the dots on each side of the panorama control. It's a little different from the pan controls in Studio One, but it works very well. You will be able to hear sounds better when they are well mixed, and you should listen to your score as you make adjustments.

BONUS SKILL: ADDING SWING

1. Open the arrangement you created in Skill Four.
2. Press Shift-G. Your cursor will be loaded with the text Swing (all). Click that text into place at the start of the arrangement. Hit Escape to unload your cursor.
3. Listen to your arrangement. All your eighth notes are now uneven. Instead of the eighth notes having even value (known as straight eighths), the first of every pair now sounds longer than the second, creating swing. Jazz players usually play eighth notes this way.
4. Click on the Swing text. It will turn orange, and a small vertical bar will appear beside the text. You can move the dot on the bar left or right with your mouse to increase or decrease the amount of swing given to the eighth notes. You can even create reverse swing by moving the dot far to the left.

As mentioned earlier in the chapter, music notation is really for composers to create music that others can play on their instruments. With Notion, you are able to print out the music as a full score for the conductor (File > Print) or as individual parts for the musicians (File > Print Parts). In the score you have created in this chapter, you have been able to write appropriate parts for instruments that normally read in different clefs (treble, alto, and bass), you have been able to write in three different types of notation (standard, guitar tab, and drum notation), and you have also written for transposing instruments. I mentioned already that the guitar is a transposing instrument, but so is the trumpet. The trumpet is pitched in B♭, meaning that it sounds a whole step lower than written. If you print out the trumpet part for this arrangement, you will find it comes out of the printer a whole step higher, in A major. When a trumpeter plays his part on a B♭ trumpet, it sounds at the correct pitch with the rest of the band.

Many years ago, you had to study all about different clefs, different notations, different transposing instruments, and so on, before you even began to compose or arrange music. While study of these is important to composers and musicians who wish to go on and make a living by composing and arranging music, it is very handy for us that Notion does so much of the work for us and lets us get on with making music quickly and efficiently.

STEAM PROBLEM SOLVING: HOW TO HEAR THINGS IN 3D— THE PANORAMA EFFECT

When you listen to a stereo recording, the music comes out of two speakers: left and right. Stereo recording uses two speakers because you have two ears. If you sit at a point equidistant from both speakers as you are listening, you should hear some sound coming from the left side and some sound coming from the right side. Interestingly, you also hear some sounds coming from the center, and from all points in between the speakers. This is because our ears work out where sound is coming from by a process of triangulation. When sound reaches our ears, the balance between what we hear in the left ear and what we hear in the right ear tells us what direction it is coming from. If we hear something equally in both ears, our brains automatically assume that it is coming from right in front of us. Therefore, if a sound is equal in both ears, our brains are tricked into thinking there is another speaker in the middle—a phenomenon we refer to as *phantom center*.

So, when we mix music, we can create the illusion that things are in different places in front of us by using the panorama effect. If we pan something totally to the left by moving the pan slider to the left, our ears tell us that the sound is coming from our left because there is a negligible amount of sound getting to our right ear. If we pan something totally to the right, our ears tell us that the sound is coming from the right because there is a negligible amount of sound getting to the left ear. If the pan fader is in the middle, both ears hear the same amount of sound, so the brain hears the sound in the phantom center. If we want to place something slightly to the left, we just move the pan fader slightly to the left; if we want to place something slightly to the right, we just move the pan fader slightly to the right.

Imagine looking at a rock band on stage. The singer is probably in the middle, so the best pan position would be center. The bass player and drummer are probably slightly left and right of center, respectively, so we would pan the bass a few degrees left and the drummer a few degrees right. The guitar player might be far to the left of the singer, so we would pan the guitar track slightly farther left than the bass, and if there's a keyboard player far to the right of the singer, we would pan the keyboard track slightly farther right than the drums. If we wanted to create the impression that the singer was moving around the stage from left to right, we would probably make quite a few changes in the panning of the singer, so that the listener's ears would get the impression of him moving around the stage.

Similarly, if a sound is coming from somewhere near you, you will hear it more loudly than if the sound is far away. In this way, if we want to make something sound like it is at the front of the stage, we make it louder. This is known as bringing the sound forward in the mix. To push a sound backward, we make it quieter.

Have you ever wondered how your cell phone can always be located when Location Services are switched on? The process is triangulation—exactly the same method that your ears use to hear sound. Your cell phone gives off a signal that pings off any cell phone towers or satellites close to you. The relative distance of your signal from each of the cell towers is what your phone's Location Services uses to pinpoint your location accurately. If your phone signal pings off only one tower, it is impossible to locate your phone definitively, only that it's somewhere on the circumference of a circle around the tower, where the radius of the circle is the distance of your phone from the tower.

So, if a person has hearing in just one ear, he or she can hear how close or far away a sound is from them due to the sound's volume but cannot hear the direction of sound.

Interestingly, one of the finest studio musicians and producers of the rock era, Brian Wilson of The Beach Boys, was mostly deaf in one ear, and therefore couldn't hear things in stereo. His recordings are often viewed as some of the greatest examples of 20th-century record production, and it is truly remarkable to listen to how he was able to overcome his hearing disability in the studio.

PROJECT B: CREATING AN ARRANGEMENT OF A TUNE FROM JOHN PLAYFORD'S *THE DANCING MASTER*

On the next page, you will find the melodies to three tunes that John Playford included in *The Dancing Master*. Choose one of these tunes and copy it into Notion. (Copying music note for note is known as *transcribing*.) Create an arrangement of the tune by adding three treble clef pitched instruments (choose a variety from guitars, brass, strings, and woodwinds), one bass clef instrument, one instrument that plays the melody as a harmony a fourth lower than the original, and one drum kit. You may include additional instruments if you wish, or add swing. Once you have made the complete arrangement, use the Virtual Mixer to pan and balance your instruments.

continued

Figure 2-9. Tunes from John Playford's *The Dancing Master* (1651).

Figure 2-9 (*continued*). Tunes from John Playford's *The Dancing Master* (1651).

HELPFUL TIPS

- Some instruments on Notion's Score Setup screen are grayed out. That means they are not available in this version of Notion, but you can purchase the sound sets for these from https://shop.presonus.com/products/notion-prods/notion-expansion-bundles. Most of these instruments are very specialist or are rarely used, so including them would increase the base price of Notion, increase the download size, and also slow the program down.
- Finish your arrangement before mixing the instruments. It may be tempting to listen and balance the mix every time you add an instrument, but it slows down the process and also tends to give

unequal weight to instruments that are added earlier in the arrangement. In any recording situation, it is always best to leave the mixing process until all instruments have been recorded.

- You can create an audio version of your arrangement by selecting File > Export Audio. Notion will create a .wav file that you can then open in iTunes or Windows Media Player. You can also upload the audio directly to http://www.soundcloud.com. You can import the audio file into Studio One later if you wish.

- While it may be cool to hear the computer play your arrangement, notation was really created for humans to read. You can print out all the parts for your arrangement (File > Print Parts) and have a group of musicians rehearse and play your arrangement.

PROJECT REQUIREMENTS CHECKLIST

Your project should include

- An accurately transcribed tune chosen from the previous pages.
- Title and composer added to the score.
- Three treble clef instruments representing a number of instrument types (guitar, brass, strings, woodwinds).
- A bass clef instrument with melody correctly transposed.
- One additional instrument with melody transposed down a perfect fourth.
- Drum part with drum patterns from the Drum Library.
- Completed arrangement panned and mixed in the Virtual Mixer.
- A written summary of your challenges and successes in completing this project.

MAKING BEATS WITH IMPACT IN STUDIO ONE 3

CHAPTER THREE GOAL AND OBJECTIVES

The goal of this chapter is to get you composing music for drums, also known as "writing beats," using the Impact drum machine in Studio One. As you read and work through the chapter, you will

- Drag and drop Impact into the Arrange view to create a new track.
- Record a kick-snare-kick-snare pattern in Impact.
- Edit, quantize, and humanize your kick-snare-kick-snare pattern.
- Record new sounds on top of the kick-snare-kick-snare pattern.
- Mix and pan drum sounds in Studio One's Mixer.
- Add compression and EQ to a drum bus.
- Create and export your own Musicloops.
- Control latency in both Studio One and Notion.

INTRODUCTION

When you begin the process of composing a new piece of music or a song, there are several different ways you can start. You could begin by writing lyrics and a melody, or you might find a set of chords that work well together in a sequence. You might get your first ideas from working out a cool riff on your guitar or your keyboard, or your inspiration might come from a catchy rhythm that you've worked out on the drums or through beat boxing. The truth is that there is no single correct way to start a composition, and many experienced and successful writers have different ways of setting out on their creative journeys. You will eventually find a method that works for you and that you feel comfortable with.

Over the next chapters, we will learn skills in recording in both Studio One and Notion, using the PS-49 MIDI Controller as well as the Audiobox USB audio interface. Whenever inspiration strikes you or you have great ideas for a song, it will be important for you to be able to get your music recorded efficiently and not struggle with trying to learn the software.

SKILL FIVE: CREATING A DRUM BEAT

Much of the music that you hear today is dependent on strong drum beats. A solid bedrock of drums in a piece of music allows people to feel the beat of a song and encourages them to move to the music, to tap their feet, or to get up and dance. Drums are the foundation on which many composers and producers choose to build their music. If the drum beats are rhythmically tight, well recorded, and strong, they will inspire many creative ideas and allow the music to grow; if the drum beats are rhythmically vague and sound weak, a composer will find it challenging to create anything over the top.

Take some time to watch a professional drum kit player. You'll see that she is using two legs and two arms at the same time, hitting all sorts of combinations of the drum pieces to establish a rhythmic groove. When you really zone in on what she is doing (and you could even ask her to show you this), you will find out that the process of drumming is really in two parts. The first part is establishing a pattern of alternating hits on the kick drum and snare drum. The kick drum and the snare drum alternate so that the kick is accenting the strong beats in the music and the snare is accenting the off beats. There is no real name for this, so we'll just refer to it throughout this chapter as the "kick-snare-kick-snare pattern." Over the kick-snare-kick-snare pattern, the drummer decorates and adds more variation using the other parts of the kit—the hi-hat, cymbals, cowbell, tambourine, woodblock, and sometimes extra kicks and snare hits. She repeats this pattern every measure, and often provides some extra decoration with a drum fill at the last of each four- or eight-measure section of the music.

Figure 3-1. Examples of a kick-snare-kick-snare pattern represented in notation.

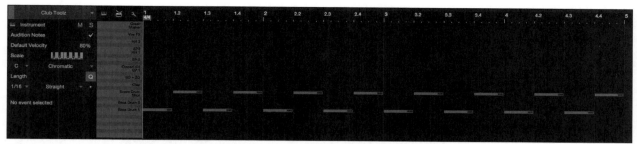

Figure 3-2. The kick-snare-kick-snare pattern from Figure 3-1 shown in Studio One's Editor.

Making beats in Studio One is fun. Even if you have little to no experience drumming or building beats, the program makes it easy to build your beats gradually and make them sound really professional. Building beats is a skill that many composers and producers work on throughout their careers, and the tools you learn by completing this chapter will get sharper as you continue to make beats.

1. Open Studio One and create a new song using the Empty Song template. Make sure the Timebase is set to Bars. Give your song a name that you will remember. You don't have to keep that title forever—you can always change it later if you like by choosing File > Save As. Open the browser if it is not already open and navigate to the Instruments tab. Inside the PreSonus folder, you will find an instrument called Impact. Click the triangle beside the name Impact (where the picture of the instrument is) and the program will reveal Impact's preset drum kit. Scroll down to the one called Club Toolz and drag it into the Arrange view. Studio One will create a new track and will draw the Impact instrument on your screen. By default, the new track will be armed for recording—the red Record button in the track header will be on.

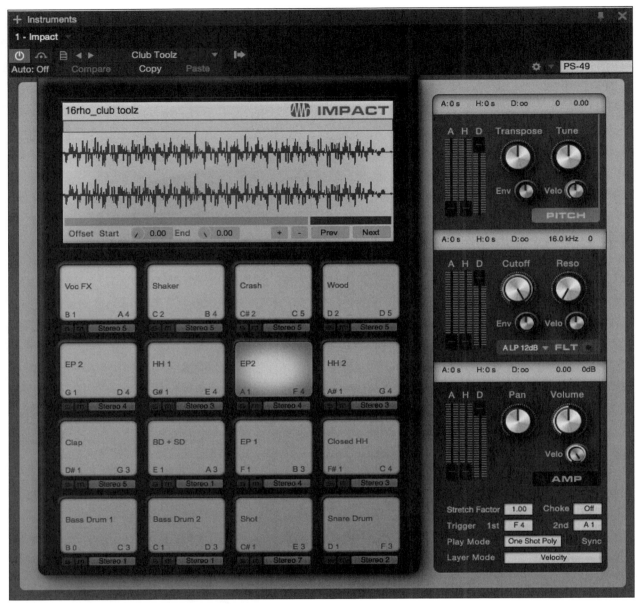

Figure 3-3. Studio One's Impact virtual drum machine.

2. Impact is a virtual instrument. This means it looks like a regular musical instrument, in this case a drum machine, but of course it is not real. The interface allows you to interact with it in a human way and enter notes into the computer. As you click on any of the 16 pads in Impact, you will hear a drum sound. You will also see that each pad shows two note names in the bottom corners. These refer to notes on your MIDI Controller. Try playing several of the keys on your MIDI Controller. You will hear drum sounds that correspond to the pads on Impact, and the

on-screen pads will light up as you press the keys. You can open and close Impact by clicking on the Instrument Editor button in the track header. The Instrument Editor button looks like a small set of piano keys. Notice that if Impact is not visible on the screen, you can still hear the sounds. Closing Impact via the Instrument Editor button does not turn the instrument off; it simply moves it out of view in case you need to see other areas of the screen.

Figure 3-4. Track Header showing the Instrument Editor button.

3. Find the Metronome controls to the right of Studio One's transport. Click on the Tempo mark and drag it downward until you get to 80 or 90 bpm. Hit C on your computer keyboard to turn the metronome on, and then click Play on the transport. (The easy way to remember this shortcut is that *C* stands for *Click*.) You will hear four clicks per measure. Try playing a kick-snare-kick-snare pattern in time with the metronome. When you think you've got that down, click Stop. If the metronome click was too fast, go ahead and slow it down to 60 or 70 bpm.

4. Click Record in the transport. Wait for four clicks and then play four measures of your kick-snare-kick-snare pattern. Click Stop. You should now have a blank measure followed by four measures of your kick-snare-kick-snare pattern in the Impact track. Hide Impact by clicking the Instrument Editor button (see Figure 3-4). Double-click the new event in the Club Toolz track to open the Editor, where you will see the notes you played, in piano-roll format. As you can see, there is a vertical representation of a piano keyboard at the left side of the Editor, and each note recorded is directly across from the note you played. Just above the vertical keyboard are two tiny icons. One looks like a bunch of piano keys, and the other looks like a drum with drum sticks. Click the drum and it will change into a listing of the pads. This probably makes reading the drum hits easier for you.

5. As you look at the notes you recorded, you will see that they probably don't line up with the grid. This is perfectly normal, and you can fix it very easily. Click on one note in the Editor and then press cmd-A (ctrl-A on a PC). All the notes will turn orange. Now press the letter Q on your computer keyboard (or select Event > Musical Functions > Quantize) and the notes will snap to the nearest sixteenth-note grid line. Q stands for *Quantize*, the term used in Music Technology to do exactly what you just did—line the notes up to a grid. Listen back to your drum beat, and you will hear that the hits are exactly in time with the metronome. If you hear that any drum hits have been quantized in the wrong direction (forward rather than backward to the beat) you can correct them individually by clicking and dragging them left or right in the Editor.

6. One of the major criticisms of quantization in music is that it makes everything sound robotic, and this is certainly true sometimes. One of the nice features of Studio One is a post-quantizing process called Humanizing. Highlight all of your notes again and select Event > Musical Functions > Humanize. Studio One now relaxes the quantization snap so that it feels a little less robotic but still sounds on the beat.

7. Studio One also has a "Humanize Less" function. You can select this by using Event > Musical Functions > Humanize Less or pressing the letter H on your computer keyboard. Humanize Less performs the same function as Humanize, but the results are not quite as marked.

8. Now we're going to overdub some more drum sounds on top of the kick-snare-kick-snare pattern. Open the Record Panel by selecting View > Record Panel. You will see it open at the bottom of the screen. Find "Takes to Layers" in the Record Mode panel and make sure it is disabled (gray). Now find "Record Mix" in the Instrument Loop Record tab and make sure it is enabled (blue). Also check that the Impact track is still armed to record. Bring Impact back into view by clicking on the Instrument Editor button in the track header. Find some hi-hat sounds (HH on the Club Toolz pads). Try playing those as you listen to the track and create an interesting rhythmic pattern. When you are ready, click Return-to-Zero and then record your hi-hats. Studio One will add your hi-hat sounds to the kick-snare-kick-snare pattern.

Highlight your notes in the Editor, quantize them, check them, and humanize them.

9. If you wish to add more drum sounds, repeat the process in step 8. Try not to do too much—the last thing you want is a drum beat that sounds like a toddler let loose on a drum kit. When you think you have created a good beat, bring the tempo back up to a faster bpm and listen. It will sound like you have mad skills at recording drums! Your loop should be exactly four measures long, between the numbers 2 and 6 on the timeline. If not, trim the front and back end of the loop by hovering over the edges of the loop in the Arrange view and dragging the sides in. Now move the loop back to the beginning of the song by clicking and dragging it. It should now be between numbers 1 and 5—these numbers are, of course, measure numbers. Save your work.

10. Go back to the Impact folder in the browser and choose a different preset than Club Toolz. Drag and drop that preset over your track in the Arrange view. Studio One will ask if you want to Load or Combine the new preset. Select Load and then listen to your beat. You will see that the pads on Impact are different and the sounds of all the drums have changed, though the beat has remained the same. Try several presets, and if you find something you prefer to Club Toolz, save your work so that the new preset saves with the song file. You can also experiment with combining presets for lots of drum sounds together.

SKILL SIX: MIXING DRUMS

Once you have a solid-sounding drum beat, it's time to mix it. Drums are a special case in the mixing phase because a drum kit is one musical instrument that is actually many individual wooden, metal, plastic, and synthetic pieces put together. Drum patterns are full of different sounds, and it takes patience and skill to mix those together so that each sound is unique yet is a valuable part of the whole. Badly mixed drums sound dull and uninteresting. Well-mixed drums provide a sparkle and energy to the music. Taking time to mix drums properly before focusing on any of the other instruments is essential to success, and something that should not be rushed.

To record drums, recording engineers usually use several microphones placed in different locations around the kit; therefore, they need several faders for the drums on a mixing console. Drums also have a large dynamic range—this means that the difference between the loudest and quietest sounds is considerable. Imagine that a drum beat is full of loud sounds such as cymbals and kick drums, but also quiet sounds such as shakers and triangle. If the engineer has to turn down the level on a fader to make the loud sounds less aggressive, he risks making the quiet sounds inaudible, and if he brings the fader on quiet instruments up for them to be heard, then he risks creating huge volume spikes because of the louder sounds.

When we mix drums, we begin by listening to each sound both on its own and with the rest of the drums to ensure that the sound has a good volume level to be heard in the mix. If we do not listen to each sound on its own, we may miss one in the mix because it is so quiet that we do not notice it past the louder drums. After establishing good volume levels, each part of the kit is placed appropriately into the horizontal plane by panning left or right, thus avoiding a mix in which the drums all sound like they are sitting on top of each other. Then the dynamic range of the whole drum kit sound is squeezed together using a *compressor*, so that quiet sounds can be boosted and loud sounds can be cut or attenuated without losing the energy of the whole drum beat. Finally, we add an *equalizer (EQ)* to highlight the important sounds in the entire drum kit and to remove any unnecessary noises.

1. Open the drum beat song that you created in Skill Five. Select the drum beat by clicking it and then hit D on the computer keyboard three times to extend your drum beat to 16 measures. D is the shortcut key for *Duplicate*, a very useful shortcut to remember.

2. Open the Mix view by clicking on the Mixer button in the bottom right of the screen. The Mix view contains a series of *channel strips* that each have a volume fader, a pan slider, and mute/solo buttons. You will see that you have maybe six or seven stereo channel strips for Impact. Do not panic—this is actually very useful for mixing the drums together. The first channel strip will have the name of the Impact preset. The rest will be numbered as Impact St 2, Impact St 3, and so on.

3. If Impact is not open, click on the Instrument Editor button. You will notice that there is an Instrument Editor button on each channel strip in the Mixer, as well as on the track header.

4. Look at the panel under each pad of Impact. You can see that each pad's sound is being sent to one of the numbered channel strips. If your kick drum is going through Stereo 1, rename that channel strip "Kick Drum" by double-clicking the label underneath the fader and typing the new name. You should also color-code this channel strip by clicking the label once. Now do the same with the Snare channel and the other channels in the Mixer.

5. If you want to route any drum sound to a different channel than the one assigned, you can do this easily by clicking the assignment at the bottom of the pad in Impact and choosing a different destination. Impact has sixteen pads routing to six or seven channel strips, so some similar sounds go to the same strip. You may find that, because of the instrument choices you made in creating your drum beat, some of your channel strips are unused, so you can reassign sounds that share a channel. For example, in Impact's Club Toolz preset, all the hi-hat sounds are assigned to Stereo 3. You may wish to change this and move one to an unused channel if you want to control the hi-hats' volume and pan separately.

6. You can hide any unused Channel Strips by ctrl-clicking (right-clicking on a PC) the channel strip and selecting Hide.

Figure 3-5. Impact channel strips labeled by drum sound.

7. Find the triangle just above the number 1 at the beginning of the timeline, at the top of the Arrange view. Click on it and drag to the right to create a cycle region. The cycle region will have two handles, one at the start of the region and one at the end. Move the end of the cycle region to the end of your 16 measures on the timeline. Click on the Cycle button (to the right of Record on the transport) to enable the cycle region. It will turn blue to show it is enabled. Now click Play and Studio One will repeat your drum beat every time it goes through the loop, until you hit Stop.

Figure 3-6. Cycle region enabled in Studio One's timeline.

8. Solo the Bass Drum channel by clicking on the S button beside the fader. Click Play on the transport and adjust the fader so that you have a good strong sound without distorting the volume. If the level is too high, a red zone will light up at the top of the fader meter. Reduce the volume and click the red region to reset it. Solo the Snare and listen to it with the Kick Drum. Adjust the volume so it is balanced with the Kick. Now click both Solo buttons again so you can hear the kick-snare-kick-snare pattern with the rest of the kit.

9. Solo another channel, adjust the fader to a good level, listen to it with the Kick and Snare, and then listen with the entire kit, always checking fader levels for balance. You should be getting very good at using Solo buttons by now.

10. Once you have balanced the levels of all the sounds in the kit, use the pan faders to separate them left to right. Leave the snare drum in the center and pan the kick five to eight degrees to the right or left. Move the hi-hats five to eight degrees to the opposite side from the kick. If you have cymbals and other instruments, place these on either side, but keep everything within 15 degrees of each side of center. Your drum kit should now sound a little more spacious in your headphones.

11. You will need to send your drum sounds to one channel so that you can add a compressor and EQ to the entire kit. We use a bus to combine the sounds of several channel strips together and create a *sub-mix*. Select the first track in the Mixer by clicking on the space below the Solo button. Now hold the Shift button and click the last track in the Mixer and you will see that all tracks are se-

lected. Click the Track menu at the top of the screen and choose Add Bus for Selected Tracks. A new channel strip appears right beside the last Impact channel strip in the Mixer. Double-click the channel's label and rename it "Impact Bus."

12. Find the Effects tab in the browser and open the PreSonus folder. Here, you will find lots of powerful tools to shape your sound as you mix. Each of these tools contains very useful presets that can help you improve the sound of your mixes as soon as you apply them. Locate the Compressor folder and expand it so you can see the folders of the compressor's presets. Open the Drums folder and look down the list until you see a preset that you think might be good. Drag that preset over the Impact Bus channel strip in the Mixer. You will see the compressor open on the screen. Listen to your mix now and see if you can hear the difference. Try another preset by dragging it onto the same bus. The new preset will replace the one you chose earlier. In this way, you can experiment with different presets and find one you like.

13. Learning to tweak the controls of the compressor is a skill in itself, but using the presets is a great way to get started with understanding what effect this tool can have on your mix. One of the outstanding aspects of Studio One is that all the presets are expertly created by the team at PreSonus, and they make marked changes to your mix as you apply them to your tracks and buses.

14. Find the Pro EQ in the Effects > PreSonus folder. Expand the Pro EQ presets and find a drum preset. Apply this in the same way as you did the compressor—by dragging it onto the Impact Bus channel strip. You should hear an immediate difference in your mix. Some EQ presets boost low sounds, some boost high sounds, and some shape the mix by a combination of both. Try some different presets until you find a good one to enhance the sound of your drums. Save your work.

15. Click the right-pointing Expand arrow above the Mute and Solo buttons in the Impact Bus channel strip. This will show you the Inserts and Sends panes for this channel, and you will see that the Compressor and Pro EQ are listed in the Inserts pane. You can bring either into view by double-clicking their respective labels, and you can turn them off or on using the Activate button beside their names. You can also open smaller graphic versions of the compressor and EQ by choosing Expand from the drop-down menu to the

left of their names. Since you already saved your work in Step 14, you can safely try tweaking the controls of the compressor and EQ to see what happens. You might find some cool tricks that you can use later as you become more experienced with mixing.

BONUS SKILL: CREATING MUSICLOOPS

1. Create a folder on your desktop titled "My Musicloops."
2. Open the Drum Beat song that you created and mixed in this chapter.
3. Cmd-click (ctrl-click on a PC) the first event in the Impact track and select Rename Events.
4. Give the event a name that you will remember, like "My Awesome Drum Beat."
5. Select the Files tab in the Studio One browser and find Desktop (it will usually be at the top of the list).
6. Expand the Desktop folder and you will see "My Musicloops" listed. Drag and drop the event you selected in Step 3 onto the folder name. Studio One will save your four-measure drum beat into this folder as a Musicloop, including an audio preview of the beat using the Impact preset you selected for it. You can now use this folder to save any Musicloops you build as you create your own music, and you can share your Musicloops with others and move them to different computers by copying the folder to a thumb drive or external hard drive.

STEAM PROBLEM SOLVING: LATENCY AND HOW TO CONTROL IT

When you record using a computer, a major issue you have to understand is latency. *Latency* is the name we give for the delay that happens between the moment you play a sound into the computer and the moment you hear it through your speakers or headphones. When you press a key on the MIDI Controller to play a sound, the computer takes a moment to process what that sound should be and then returns that to your headphones. Also, when you record through the audio interface, it takes the computer a moment to process the sound into a digital form, add any volume, panning, or digital effects that you have inserted onto the track, and then return that to your headphones. The result is a tiny but inevitable delay between the sound you create and the sound you hear.

You may have noticed latency while working on Skill One. If the Mixer dial is turned toward Playback as you speak into the microphone, you can hear a slight delay in your voice. This is because you are hearing the sound after it has already been through the computer. The Mixer dial is there to help you overcome this problem. When the Mixer dial is turned to Inputs, you hear the sound passed directly to your headphones, before it gets processed by the computer. Therefore, you hear no latency. If you have the Mixer dial placed somewhere between Playback and Inputs, you might hear two versions of your own voice. This difference becomes even more noticeable if you are using monitor speakers rather than headphones and there is a considerable distance between you and the speakers.

When you are recording spoken voice, latency is not usually an issue unless it is very marked, but when you are trying to perform music, where rhythmic accuracy is required, any delay at all makes recording difficult. Consider a situation in which a singer is trying to record a vocal over pre-recorded backing music. She would need to hear the backing music through her headphones, and she might also prefer to hear her voice returned to her with reverb added, so the option of turning the Mixer dial all the way to Inputs would not help her at all. Turning the mixer dial halfway to Playback would give her two versions of her voice, and turning the dial all the way to Playback would mean she would hear the backing tracks and reverb later than when she's actually singing. Therefore, we need some other method of controlling latency.

There are a number of ways to keep latency at bay. First, make sure you have no other programs running when Studio One or Notion are open, as other programs will slow down the computer's processing speed and increase latency. It is also a good idea to restart your computer before embarking on a recording project, to clear out the cache and any bad sectors in working memory.

Both Studio One and Notion use a buffer to process the sound while you are playing it. This buffer holds samples of the incoming information and releases it in bursts to be processed, and the size of the buffer has an important impact on latency. If the buffer size is small, sound will get processed more quickly and there will be less delay. However, a small buffer can sometimes result in analog sound being inadequately translated into digital sound, and an annoying static can be heard. If the buffer size is large, there is much less risk of static sound, but the length of time between the buffer's bursts of information creates more delay. You should know how to adjust the buffer size in both Studio One and Notion and keep it at the smallest size required for your work without hearing static. If you do begin to hear static, particularly during a long recording session, it is usually best to save your work and restart the computer before adjusting the buffer size. If the restart does not fix the static problem, then you should increase the buffer size up to the next option available.

Latency is usually less of an issue when recording using a MIDI Controller, as computers process MIDI data very quickly, but it still can become an issue if there is a noticeable delay between the moment you strike a key and the moment you hear the sound that key triggers. You can usually employ a smaller buffer size for MIDI recording than you can for live audio.

In Studio One, you will find the buffer size settings in the Audio Setup screen, which you can access from the Start page or from Studio One > Preferences. Look for the box marked Device Block Size; this will tell you what the current buffer size is, measured in samples. You can click on that number to change it, and as you increase the size of the buffer, you will see an increase in the measurements of Input Latency and Output Latency in the boxes below.

Figure 3-7. Audio Setup screen in Studio One.

In Notion, you will be able to adjust the buffer size via a slider found on the Audio tab under Notion > Preferences.

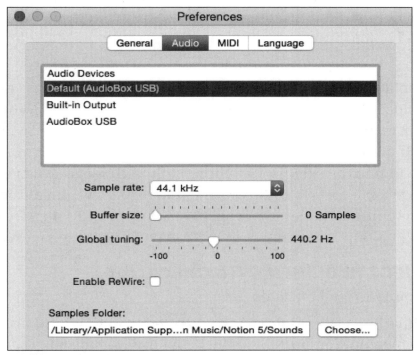

Figure 3-8. Audio tab in Notion.

PROJECT C: COMPOSING MUSIC WITH BEATS

In this project, you should use the skills you learned in Chapter Three to create a song using nothing but drum beats. You should record three eight-measure beats (beat A, beat B, and beat C) using different preset drum kits in Impact. You should arrange them in this order:

Measures:	1–8	9–16	17–24	25–32	33-40
Beat:	A	B	A	C	A

After all your beats are recorded, you should mix everything appropriately.

HELPFUL TIPS

- Create three Impact tracks in Studio One. Label them Beat A, Beat B, and Beat C.
- Each Impact track should use a different preset.

- Create each beat individually. Mute the tracks you are not using while you record your beats. When you have recorded all three beats, you can arrange then into ABACA order on the timeline.
- Remember to quantize and humanize each beat after you have recorded it.
- Remember that you can press the letter D on your keyboard to duplicate an event in Studio One, and you can copy an event by holding the cmd key (ctrl on a PC) and dragging the event to a new position.
- It is essential that you color-code the Impact tracks as you add them into the Arrange view, because Studio One will then color-code them automatically for you in the Mix view. Since each Impact instrument has five or six channel strips each, the Mix view will become very difficult to use if everything is the same color.

PROJECT REQUIREMENTS CHECKLIST

Your project should include

- Three beats labeled **Beat A**, **Beat B**, and **Beat C**.
- 40 measures.
- Beats arranged in the sequence ABACA.
- Properly recorded, quantized, humanized, and mixed beats.
- Effective use of compression and EQ.
- Color-coded and properly titled tracks.
- A written summary of your challenges and successes in completing this project.

USING CHORDS
IN NOTION

4

CHAPTER FOUR GOAL AND OBJECTIVES

The goal of this chapter is to get you composing music in Notion using a repeating diatonic chord sequence. As you read and work through the chapter, you will

- Construct diatonic chords.
- Construct chord inversions.
- Create a chord sequence using block chords.
- Create a chord sequence using broken chords.
- Construct chords in similar and contrary motion.
- Compose and record a melody.
- Prepare a score and parts for performance.
- Trace the history of sheet music printing.

INTRODUCTION

This chapter is all about using chords to create the framework for a piece of music. A *chord* is any group of three or more notes that sound good together. Chords are used to harmonize melodies and are essential building blocks of music composition. When you place different chords together one after the other, you create a *chord sequence*. Repeating chord sequences or stringing different chord sequences together creates structure for the music. For example, a song might have a specific eight-measure chord sequence for a verse that is then repeated for a second verse, followed by a new chord sequence for a chorus. After that, the music may go back to the verse chord sequence, then to the chorus sequence again, and then maybe to a new chord sequence for a bridge. If there is a guitar solo or keyboard solo, the soloist would improvise over the chords of one of those chord sequences.

Within any key, there is a naturally occurring set of *diatonic* chords that can be made using the notes of the scale. For example, find the notes of the C major scale on your MIDI Controller by going to any C note and then pressing each of the white notes up to the next C. These eight notes are the notes in the scale of C major (there are no flats or sharps in C, so you don't need to use the black notes). Now place the thumb of your right hand on a C note and place your fingers over the next four notes, D, E, F, and G. Now press down the notes under your thumb, middle finger, and pinkie. You should be holding down the notes C, E, and G—these are the first, third, and fifth notes of the scale, forming the chord of C major. This is known as the tonic or I chord (with I being used as the Roman numeral for the number 1).

Move your hand up so that your thumb is on F and play F, A, and C. This is the F or IV chord. Move your hand up one key to G and play the G chord, also known as V, using the notes G, B, and D. These three chords, I, IV, and V, are used in hundreds of songs in the key of C major, and you can certainly use them to make many great chord sequences.

I, IV, and V are all *major* chords—they sound bright. There are three *minor* chords in the key of C—these sound darker than the major chords. These are the chords of D minor (D, F, A), E minor (E, G, B) and A minor (A, C, E). We use lowercase Roman numerals for those chords: D minor is ii, E minor is iii, A minor is vi.

There is one more chord in the key of C major. The chord formed using B, D, and F is a diminished chord and sounds uncertain. We use the lowercase Roman numeral for 7 followed by a small circle to denote this chord (vii°).

When we write these seven chords on the staff, they look like this:

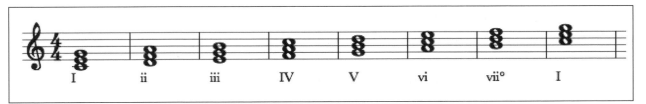

I   ii   iii   IV   V   vi   vii°   I

Figure 4-1. Diatonic chords in C major.

When the chords are written in this way, they are in closed position. The distance between the lowest and highest notes in the chord is as small as possible. Even if you play a chord with the notes in different places, it is still the same chord, though it may no longer be in closed position. The following chords are all C major chords because they contain the notes C, E, and G.

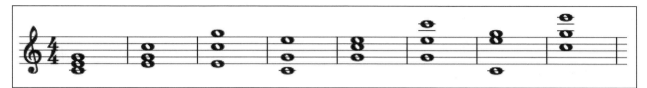

Figure 4-2. Several different C major chords.

If the lowest note in the chord is the same as the name of the chord, then the chord is in *root position*. If the lowest note is the third note of the scale, then the chord is in *first inversion*. If the lowest note is the fifth of the scale, then the chord is in *second inversion*.

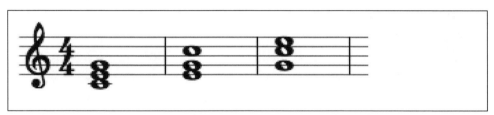

Figure 4-3. C major chord in root position, first inversion, and second inversion.

SKILL SEVEN: COMPOSING A PIECE OF MUSIC WITH A REPEATING CHORD SEQUENCE

Many pieces of music are composed over a repeating chord sequence. A set of four to eight chords repeated gives a good foundation for a melody to be added over the top. Many times, as you listen to music composed in this way, you get a sense of knowing or predicting where the music will go next. This is natural, and part of the attraction of composing this way. One of the most famous examples of a repeating chord structure is Johann Pachelbel's Canon in D, which is often played at weddings and is a frequent favorite on classical music radio stations. Pachelbel wrote his Canon in D for string orchestra. In the music, he establishes an eight-measure chord sequence over a repeating bass line played by cellos and double basses. Violas and second violins fill out the chords, and the first violins provide many variations of melody over the chord sequence as the music develops.

Other examples of music in which chord sequences repeat might be any jazz blues tune, such as Duke Ellington's "C Jam Blues" and Charlie Parker's "Billie's Bounce," or popular songs, such as "Jolene" by Dolly Parton, "Stand By Me" by Ben E. King, and "All Along the Watchtower" by Bob Dylan.

1. Open Notion and create a New Score. From the Keyboards/Harp category, choose either a Piano or Electric Piano. Click on Exit Score Setup. Give your new song a name (you can change it later if you change your mind), enter your name as the composer, and add the date.

2. Try playing some chords on your MIDI Controller. You should hear them through your headphones. Use notes in the upper half of the keyboard, from C3 upward. Try playing different chords one after another and make a mental note of chords that sound good in sequence.

3. Click on the piano keyboard icon in the Toolbar at the top right of the screen, and you will see the on-screen virtual keyboard appear under the entry palette. Now, as you play chords on the MIDI Controller, you will see the corresponding notes turn gray on the on-screen keyboard. Note that there is a numbering discrepancy between the MIDI Controller and the on-screen keyboard—notes C3 to B3 show up in the C4 octave in Notion. So long as you are aware that this happens, you won't find it confusing.

4. Select a quarter note from the entry palette, click on the top staff of the piano part (it will turn yellow), and then click the pencil icon on the virtual keyboard to enable note writing.

5. Play four C chords on your MIDI Controller. You will see them show up in the score. Play a different chord four times for measure 2, and select another chord for measure 3. Try using different inversions as well as some root position chords. Keep going until you've completed eight measures (but make sure you use another C chord for measure 8). If at any point you make a mistake, just press cmd-Z (ctrl-Z on a PC) to undo your last chord. Remember to save your work.

6. Click the pencil icon on the virtual keyboard again to turn off note writing, select the first measure of the lower staff in the score, click on the pencil again, and now add a bass line. To do

this, enter the root note of each chord as four quarter notes in each measure. Turn off note writing again and listen to your eight-measure chord sequence.

7. Your chord sequence will sound strong if your bass line and the top notes of your chords move in contrary motion. *Contrary motion* means that if the top note of the chord moves up from measure to measure, the bass line goes down, and if the top note of the chord goes down, the bass line goes up. Look through your chord sequence and see if you can find any examples of similar motion between chords and bass. One way you can fix this is by changing the bass note. Move the last two bass notes of the measure preceding the similar motion, either to a different note in the chord or to a different octave of the same note, so that you achieve contrary motion instead.

8. Go to the Score Setup screen and add a guitar to your score. Exit Score Setup. Choose an eighth note from the entry palette and turn note writing back on by clicking the virtual keyboard's pencil icon. Now enter the same chord sequence in the guitar part by playing broken chords. This means you're going to play the notes of the chords individually in sequence. If the piano chord is C, E, G from bottom to top, try playing C E G E C E G E as eighth notes for the guitar part. When you've completed all eight measures, listen to your work.

9. Add some more instruments from the Score Setup screen and add your chord sequence to these other instruments, either as chords played together, broken chords, or bass lines. Feel free to experiment with how you orchestrate your chord sequence; use combinations of high and low instruments, try some whole-note or half-note chords, add some broken chords in sixteenth notes or thirty-second notes. You can't really know if something sounds good or not unless you are willing to have fun, be creative, and listen to your work as you go.

10. When you have added several more instruments and are happy with the sound of your chord sequence, select all eight measures by dragging from above the first note in the top staff to below the last note in the bottom staff. Notion will highlight the measures. Select Duplicate from the Edit menu and duplicate your chord sequence three times, giving you 32 total measures. The shortcut for Duplicate is cmd-D (ctrl-D on a PC).

11. You will need to add a measure at the end of your score for a final chord. Move your score so you can see the last measure (measure 32). Press the letter I on your keyboard, and your cursor will become a bar line. Click in any staff after the last note of the music and an extra measure will be added. Now add a whole note C chord (C, E, G) to the last measure. At this point, it would be a good idea to save your work.

12. Return to the Score Setup Screen and add a melody instrument to your song. Choose a flute, clarinet, oboe, trumpet, or violin. Exit Score Setup and select your melody instrument by clicking on it.

13. You are now going to create a melody for your repeating chord sequence. Your first thought might be "but how will I know what notes to play?" and this is certainly a question all composers think about when they start to write melodies. Since your music is in the key of C and you have used no sharps or flats, any note in the scale of C will blend nicely with your chord sequence. Click Play on the transport and see if you can hear where you think a melody might fit in. Try improvising by making up melodies on the keyboard, using only the white keys. Make sure you are playing one note at a time (most melody instruments cannot play two notes at once, let alone chords). Listen to your chord sequence as many times as it takes to find your melody—this is the most important creative part of this compositional skill.

14. When you are ready, return to the beginning of your song and click Record on the transport. In the dialog box that appears, you can set options for Metronome Click and Count-off, though you probably don't need these because your chords are in even quarter notes, so you should be able to record with those chords giving you your tempo. Click on Start Recording. Let the chord sequence play through the first eight measures, and then begin to record your melody at measure 9. You may like to continue improvising and recording melody throughout all the measures of the song, gradually getting more complex as you go, or you may choose to compose eight or sixteen measures and then repeat those measures through the rest of the song using copy-and-paste.

15. Listen to your music the whole way through. You will hear how Notion chooses to play your melody with the exact inflections

you played when you recorded it. Every note you played softly is played softly when you listen back, and every note you played loudly is returned loudly. This provides a human feel to the music—it sounds exactly as you, the musician, played it. You can turn off this feature if you like. Click in the first measure of the melody line and choose Edit > Select Part followed by Tools > Clear Velocities.

16. Save your work.

SKILL EIGHT: PREPARING YOUR SCORE FOR PERFORMANCE

One of the advantages of using notation software on a computer is that you can print out your music and give it to people to play on their instruments or to sing. It is always magical to hear your music played by others or to be a part of that performance.

If you want to rehearse and perform your music, each member of the ensemble will need his or her own *part*. A part is simply a version of the music with just their notes on it. A conductor will need the *full score* in which all the parts are included. Notion allows you to print out both the full score and the individual parts easily.

Before you print out your music, you will need to add some directions for the players. These include dynamic markings (*piano*, *forte*, and so on), slurs and articulation markings, tempo indications, and sometimes lyrics for singers.

1. Open the composition you created in Skill Seven.
2. When you created your song, you will have noticed that a tempo marking was placed at the beginning of the score. This tells you the speed of the music in quarter-note beats per minute, or bpm. You will also see that this tempo marking has been repeated every eighth measure because you duplicated the first eight measures. Go ahead and delete the tempo markings at measures 9, 17, and 25 by clicking on each tempo mark to select it and then pressing the delete key. You can also change the speed of your music by double-clicking the tempo mark at measure 1 and entering a new bpm marking.
3. Notion will automatically print the tempo marking on each part, though it is not usual for printed parts to contain a tempo marking in bpm. It is more usual to have a description of the

speed. Select the tempo marking at measure 1 and then select Edit > Hide to hide it.

4. Click on the leftmost tab of the entry palette—the Text Entry tab. Select Text from the submenu. Your cursor will change to the word TEXT. Now click above the first measure in the score and type a tempo description for your composition. You can use an Italian term (*allegro, moderato, lento,* and so on) or an English term (*fast, moderate, slow,* and so on). You can also use an appropriate term in a language of your choice; if your performers all speak Spanish, use a Spanish term. You must add the text marking to each instrument in your score so that it will print on the individual parts. For an instrument that has two staves, such as the piano or guitar, you only need to add the tempo description above the upper part.

5. You can add rehearsal letters from the Text Entry tab. Rehearsal letters allow a conductor to specify a place in the score easily during a rehearsal. Choose the submenu item that has a box around the letter A and add rehearsal letters above the top line of your score, ideally right over the bar lines at the beginning of measures 9, 17, and 25. You do not need to put these rehearsal letters on each instrument—Notion automatically adds them to the parts.

6. While you're still working with the Text Entry tab, you'll see that the rightmost two options allow you to add chord letters or diagrams. Although these are not strictly necessary for this score, since all the notes are already written out, you might like to try adding chords to the piano and/or guitar parts, especially if you are a guitar player. You can also try adding lyrics if you would like your melody to be sung instead of played on an instrument. Note that anything you add from the text panel is for human performers only. The computer will not be able to interpret guitar chords, lyrics, or tempo descriptions. The computer already has the information it needs to play the music with the notes and the bpm markings.

7. The fifth tab on the entry palette is the Dynamics tab. From here you can add crescendos, diminuendos, and other dynamic markings. Try adding a *pianissimo* mark to your score by selecting the *pp*. As you hover over the score, you will see a gray vertical line that runs from the top to the bottom of the music.

One staff will be highlighted in white—this is the part that your *pp* mark will apply to. Click on the score to add your dynamic marking. You will see that your cursor is still loaded with *pp* until you hit Escape. This allows you to place more *pp* markings in your score quickly and easily. Add crescendos and diminuendos using the hairpin symbols. When you add a hairpin, you need to click once where you want the hairpin to start and once where you want it to end.

8. Dynamic markings should be added to every instrument in the score. This will allow you to have different instruments play at different volumes, to help balance the music. Remember that a marking of *forte* on a trumpet is very different from *forte* on a flute or violin. You may also want to have your chordal and bass instruments get quieter when the melody starts.

9. Slurs, accents, and other articulation markings can be entered from the fourth of the entry palette tabs. Slurs are entered in the same way as crescendos and diminuendos, with a click to begin the slur and another click to end the slur.

10. Look through the other tabs in the entry palette. You will find other musical items that you may want to add to your score or to the individual parts, such as rallentando or ritardando marks, fermatas, ornaments, and so on. You will find that adding these to your music is quite intuitive. Techniques for individual instruments can be added from the rightmost tab of the entry palette. The technique markings available will depend on what instrument is currently selected in the score.

11. You can make alterations to font sizes and types from the Score menu, much as you would with a word processor. The default settings for Notion produce high-quality parts and score, so you will usually not need to make any changes. However, it is good to know that these options exist if, for example, you need to print a part in larger type size for a musician who has vision challenges.

12. When you are satisfied that you have added appropriate markings to your score so that your performers will know how you want them to play, choose File > Print and File > Print Parts to send your music to the printer. Now you can go rehearse your music and schedule a performance.

BONUS SKILL: EXPORTING YOUR SONG FROM NOTION

Maybe you have decided you want some friends to play your song, and you have printed out parts for them to rehearse. You might also like to send them a copy of the music that they can listen to. You could send them a copy of the Notion file, but they would not be able to listen to that (unless they also own a copy of Notion). Instead, you need to send them an audio version of the song or send them a link to a version of the song online. You might also like to create an audio version of your song so that you can import it into Studio One and add some other drum beats and effects. Notion allows you to do all of this quite easily.

1. Open the file you created in Skill Eight.
2. Choose Export Audio... from the File menu.
3. The Export Audio dialog box allows you to specify where to save your audio file. Choose a place on your computer that you can find easily (the Desktop is always a good idea).
4. The Export Audio dialog box default settings for audio are ideal. Your song will export at 16-bit audio quality, it will render the audio offline, and it will use the Master output as the sound source. Leave these settings exactly as they are and click on OK.
5. Notion will now create an audio file of your song. It will have the same name as your Notion file but will end with a .wav extension. You can now move or copy this audio file to a flash drive, send it via email, or upload it to a personal website.
6. Notion allows you to export your song directly to http://www. soundcloud.com, and if you have an account there, you could certainly send friends a direct link to your song on Soundcloud. You can also export your songs to http://www.nimbit.com, a free service hosted by PreSonus where you can store and even sell your music.
7. To import your audio into Studio One, create a new song with the same bpm as your Notion file and then drag your .wav file directly into the Arrange view. Now it could be fun to "remix" your song by adding drum beats or Musicloops.

Special note: The size of your audio file will be proportional to the length of your song (approximately 10MB per minute of audio).

If your email client or upload service has difficulty with the file size, you will need to convert your song to an mp3 version. You need to use a separate utility such as the one at http://audioformat.com to convert the .wav file to an .mp3. Studio One offers this capability as a program extension that you can purchase from the PreSonus website (https://shop.presonus.com/products/studio-one-prods/studio-one-add-ons).

STEAM PROBLEM SOLVING: PRODUCING LARGE QUANTITIES OF SHEET MUSIC

Musicians make money from live performances and also from the sale of copies of their music. The ability to produce multiple copies quickly has been essential to the musical world for many hundreds of years. Before the invention of the printing press, all music was copied by hand. Copyists would spend many hours writing music on staff paper for others to play, as there was really no other way for music to be duplicated. Most of the music copied in this way was written for the church; secular music was usually taught aurally from teacher to pupil and rarely written down. For this reason, we have considerable evidence today of what ancient sacred music sounded like, but not so much of secular music.

Printing, or the ability to create an impression in ink on a piece of paper, was developed during the middle of the 15th century. At first, plates would be engraved with a reverse image of the intended text, and they would then be brushed with ink and pressed onto blank sheets of paper. Moveable type, where text could be written line-by-line, very much sped up the printing process and was less expensive and less wasteful. Many of the first printed documents were Bibles, and somewhat later, the printing presses were used to duplicate sacred choral music.

It was important to print multiple copies of music so every member of a choir had access to the score, so printers worked to find a way to reproduce sheet music effectively. Two major methods emerged in the 16th century: the Petrucci method, in which music was printed in three passes through the machine (staves, notes, and then lyrics), and the Rastell method, in which each individual character contained the staff, note, and lyric. The Rastell method was the less expensive of the two and so was adopted more commonly, but you can often see in Rastell printing that there are breaks between staffs, and sometimes they do not quite line up correctly. The example from Playford's book shown in Chapter Two (see Figure 2-1) was printed using the Rastell method.

By the end of the 18th century, professional publishing houses in central Europe specialized in the production and sale of sheet music, and this accounts for much of the dominance of central European music during the 19th century. Breitkopf and Härtel Publishers in Leipzig, Germany, published the music of many German and Austrian composers, including Beethoven, Haydn, and Mozart. Schott Music in Mainz, Germany, published operas by many French and Italian composers.

By the 20th century, publishing houses throughout Europe and North America were publishing music. Many composers were able to make a living through sales of sheet music. However, the dawn of recording meant that the medium by which music was sold changed radically. By the mid-1950s, record sales overtook sheet music sales, and composers became more dependent on the sales of recordings of their work rather than on printed copies. Today, musicians rely on CD sales and downloads for their income, though publishers such as Hal Leonard still make it possible for us to go to the store and buy a copy of the music that we can play at home on a piano or other instrument. Hal Leonard is one of a number of publishers who also offer online sales, where you can purchase a pdf copy of sheet music on the Internet. The advantage of this method is that you can often specify what key you want your music in, and even sometimes specify the instrumentation of the arrangement. You can usually also hear the arrangement before you purchase it. With an iPad app such as Hal Leonard's Sheet Music Direct, you can even download sheet music to your mobile device so that you can play it from the screen, meaning you don't necessarily need to print the music after you've purchased it.

Figure 4-4. Hal Leonard's Sheet Music Direct app.

PROJECT D: COMPOSING MUSIC WITH A REPEATING CHORD SEQUENCE

In this project, you should use the skills you learned in Chapter Four to create a song using a repeating chord sequence. You should either export your song as a .wav file for others to hear or have live musicians perform it.

HELPFUL TIPS

- Take time to work on the chord sequence. Listen to it several times to make sure you like it. It is a lot of work to change the chord sequence once you have already added other instruments and melody.
- Choose to write either block chords or broken chords by listening to how they sound on the instrument. Some instruments are more suited to different types of chords and chord voicings.

You can always write a measure or two and listen to it before you commit.

- As you improvise a melody, remember that there are no mistakes—only choices. You can always undo your recording and record again.
- Slowing the tempo of the song before you record can really help.
- Tempo indications apply to the whole score. Dynamic indications refer only to the part they are written on.
- If a performer has difficulty reading a part because of where the dynamics or other text items are, it is your job to fix it. It is easy to edit in Notion and move items around. Regard it as part of the learning journey, not an obstacle, and always be willing to improve your printed music layout as well as the actual notes you hear.

PROJECT REQUIREMENTS CHECKLIST

Your project should include

- An eight-measure chord sequence in C major, using only diatonic chords.
- One chord per measure.
- At least four repetitions of the chord sequence.
- A final chord of C major.
- A bass line that moves in contrary motion to the top notes of the chord sequence.
- Combinations of block chords and broken chords.
- At least four instruments gradually adding chords through the song.
- Melody played on at least one instrument.
- Properly formatted score with tempo indications and dynamic markings.
- A written summary of your challenges and successes in completing this project.

CREATING ELECTRONIC MUSIC WITH VIRTUAL INSTRUMENTS IN STUDIO ONE

5

CHAPTER FIVE GOAL AND OBJECTIVES

The goal of this chapter is to make you familiar with all of the virtual instruments included in Studio One—Mojito, Mai Tai, Presence, Impact, and Sample One. As you read and work through the chapter, you will

- Open a virtual instrument in Studio One.
- Manipulate oscillators, filters, amps, and envelopes.
- Create and save new presets in virtual instruments.
- Control synth parameters using the rotary dials on the PS-49 controller.
- Write automation for any synth parameter.
- Compose electronic music in binary form using layered soft synth sounds.
- Transpose notes in soft synths.
- Understand and appreciate the contributions of Léon Theremin and Robert Moog, and trace the development of the first electronic instruments.
- Compose a piece of electronic music in ternary form using multiple virtual instruments.

INTRODUCTION

In Chapter Four, we created a composition suitable for performance by acoustic instruments. Notation software such as Notion is very good for exactly this purpose—composing music for humans to perform. Notion allows us to write, edit, and refine our music just as humans have done on paper for centuries, but now with the help of the computer. Printing out the music, rehearsing it, and performing it live are all vital parts of the creative process.

While it is certainly possible to compose electronic music using Notion, it is not really what the software was written for. Modern instruments such as synthesizers and drum machines are capable of many more sounds and subtleties of performance than can be written down in notation. A Digital Audio Workstation (DAW) like Studio One gives us an ideal environment in which to compose electronic music because we can record the music, edit it, and refine it using the included synthesizers and other instruments, which we call *virtual instruments*.

Virtual instruments, also known as *software synthesizers* or simply *soft synths*, are included as plug-ins with every major DAW package on the market. Studio One includes five of them—Impact (which you used in Chapter Three), Mai Tai, Mojito, Presence, and Sample One. Just like any synthesizer that you can buy in a music store, these virtual instruments contain many different sounds to choose from and many ways to alter the sounds. However, unlike hardware synths, the virtual instrument exists only as a picture of the instrument within the software, with sliders, rotary dials, faders, and other buttons to allow you to alter the parameters of the instrument. You can play the notes on the instrument either by clicking on keys or pads on the screen or by using a MIDI Controller such as the PreSonus PS-49 included with the *Music Creation Suite*. Sometimes, you can also control the onscreen sliders and rotary dials with similar sliders and rotary dials if you have them on your MIDI Controller. At the top left of the PS-49 controller, you will see four rotary dials, labeled **C1**, **C2**, **C3**, and **C4**, and we will learn how to set these up to control soft synth parameters as we work through Skill Nine.

SKILL NINE: WORKING WITH MOJITO

1. Open Studio One and create a new song.
2. Find the Instruments tab in the browser and open the folder called PreSonus. Inside, you will find folders for Impact, Mai Tai, Mojito, Presence, and Sample One. Open Mojito, and you will see many of Mojito's preset instruments. Choose one that appeals to you and drag the preset into the Arrange view in Studio One. The program will create a new track for you and draw the Mojito virtual instrument. Mojito is the simplest of the virtual instruments in Studio One, so it's best to learn how to use it before moving on to the other soft synths. Once you understand how to load a preset,

what various parameters such as oscillators, filters, and amps are, how to record and automate sounds through the synth, and how to adjust controls using rotary dials, you will be able to transfer these skills to Mai Tai, Presence, Impact, and Sample One.

3. Play some notes on your MIDI Controller. You should be able to hear Mojito in your headphones. You can change the sound loaded into Mojito by double-clicking on any of the other presets listed in the Mojito browser folder.

Figure 5-1. Mojito's graphical user interface.

4. Mojito is a *monophonic* synthesizer. This means you will be able to play only one note at a time; you will not be able to play chords. Monophonic synths have some very cool properties and are often used for lead lines and bass lines. Try playing two keys at once on your MIDI Controller, or try holding one key down and pressing other keys. You will hear how a monophonic synth is different from a regular piano or other keyboard instrument.

5. One of the great things about Mojito is the portamento function that adds glide to notes as you move between them. Find the dial labeled **Porta** in the bottom left of Mojito. You can increase the length of portamento (glide) by moving the rotary dial clockwise with your mouse, and you can choose from three modes—legato, retrigger, and off—by clicking the box above the rotary dial. Experiment with these modes and the portamento timing as you move from note to note on your MIDI Controller. You should be able to hear differences in the glide effect.

6. Beside the Portamento section of Mojito, you will find the AMP. The Gain control affects the amount of volume boost given to the sound, and the Velo dial beside it controls how much the gain is controlled by the velocity, or pressure, with which you press keys on your MIDI Controller. The ADSR controls regulate the *envelope* of the sound. You will also see ADSR controls in Presence and other soft synths. The envelope of the sound is simply the shape of the note from beginning to finish. The A fader controls the rate of attack from fast (at the bottom of the fader throw) to slow (at the top of the fader throw). The D fader controls the length of decay after the initial attack, from short to long. The S fader controls the sustain of the note, or how loud the note is after the attack and decay phases, from quiet to loud. The R fader controls how quickly the note fades away after you release the MIDI Controller key, from quick to slow. Try experimenting with the AMP settings as you play notes on your MIDI Controller.

7. In the top left of Mojito, you will find the OSC section. This controls the shape and rate of the *oscillator* that generates the sound of the instrument. An oscillator is simply an electronic device that generates a sound signal by moving sound waves. Sound waves are created by the speeding up of sound pressure toward you (*compression*) followed by the slowing of the pressure (*rarefaction*). The speed of the sound wave produced and the quality of the wave are the most important aspects of sound synthesis. A sine wave, in which the sound wave moves smoothly between its compression and rarefaction stages, is a pure sound. When the sound becomes more angular, such as that produced by a triangle wave or square wave, the sound becomes harsher. Mojito's oscillator dials allow you to choose between a sawtooth wave and a pulse wave, both of which produce very rich sounds. You can also control the pitch of the oscillator and the speed at which it modulates by using an additional LFO, or low-frequency oscillator. The SubOSC dial allows you to bring in a second oscillator pitched one octave below. Again, you should experiment with the dials in the OSC section as you play notes on your MIDI Controller.

8. The FLT section of Mojito controls how many frequencies are filtered out of the sound. The most important dial is the Cutoff; it controls the point at which treble frequencies are filtered out

of the notes that you hear. As the Cutoff dial is moved clockwise, the sound of Mojito becomes brighter. The Resonance dial adds extra frequencies around and over the Cutoff and is capable of some exciting effects. In addition, you will see filter controls that affect the filter LFO, the envelope, the drive, and the velocity. The best way to learn what these dials do is to experiment as you continue to play sounds on your MIDI Controller.

9. The FX section in the bottom right of Mojito controls a modulation parameter, which lets you add color to the sound, ranging from a gentle chorus effect to a heavy flanger. The LFO in this section is controlled by the LFO in the FLT section above.

10. At this point, you should spend some time loading different presets and altering the parameters of Mojito to find some new sounds. The best way to get to know any synth is to play with it a lot and find sounds that maybe nobody has ever heard before.

11. As you load any preset in Mojito and alter its parameters, you will notice that an asterisk appears beside the preset name in the Mojito interface. You can save the changes to the preset or create a new preset by clicking the Clipboard icon to the left of the preset name, just past the horizontal arrows. Choose Store Preset to write a new preset or Replace Preset to overwrite the current one.

Figure 5-2. Creating presets in Mojito.

12. Click Record in the transport section of Studio One and record some notes from your MIDI Controller in the Mojito track. Once you have finished recording, click on Stop, create a cycle region

around the event you recorded, and enable the Cycle Loop. If you don't remember how to do this, refer to the seventh step of Skill Six in Chapter Three.

13. Click Play and try shaping the sound by altering Mojito's parameters as you listen. You can also double-click any preset in the Mojito browser folder and replace the current preset setting of Mojito while the track is playing. Notice that as you do this, the notes do not disappear, because they are recorded in the track, not in the virtual instrument. In fact, if you were to replace Mojito with a different soft synth, such as Presence, the notes would play in the new instrument instead.

14. On the top left of your PS-49 MIDI Controller are four physical rotary dials marked C1 through C4. Each of these is mapped to a control in Mojito by default. Move C1 left to right and you will see the FLT Cutoff move on screen. C2 is mapped to FLT Resonance, C3 controls the FLT envelope, and C4 operates the AMP Decay fader. The volume slider on the PS-49 controls the AMP Gain. Pretty cool, huh?

15. Now ctrl-click (right-click on a PC) on the large Cutoff dial in Mojito and select Edit Filter Cutoff Automation. Studio One will add a track underneath the Mojito track in the Arrange view. You can rename this track by double-clicking the name in the track pane. You will see a vertical line through this new track. Using the Arrow tool (you'll find that in the tool pane at the top of Studio One), you can create hit points along this line by clicking on it and then dragging these hit points up and down to create automation—this is known as drawing automation. Listen to the track again and watch the Cutoff dial while you listen to the effect. You can automate any control in Mojito exactly the same way.

16. Notice that there is a box labeled **Read** to the left of the name of your new automation lane. This is the automation mode indicator, and right now it is set to read the automation you have drawn. By clicking on the automation mode indicator, you can change the current mode. You can turn the automation off if you wish, or you can write automation yourself by playing the track and moving the assigned control in Mojito. Touch mode allows you to make small changes to the automation—rather than overwrite the entire automation track. Studio One will write automation only for the moments when you are moving

the fader or rotary dial. Latch mode will do the same thing, except it will retain the setting you leave on the fader or dial rather than return to what was already written. Be careful using these modes, and take time to get used to what they all do. Remember, you can undo your automation with cmd-Z (ctrl-Z on a PC) if necessary. You should always return the automation mode to Read after you have done any editing or writing of automation.

Once you are comfortable with loading presets and shaping sounds using oscillators, filters, and amp settings in Mojito, you should try playing with Mai Tai, Presence, and Sample One. You load each of these synths into Studio One by dragging and dropping a preset from the browser into the Arrange view. Both Mojito and Mai Tai are synthesizers—they create sounds through manipulation of oscillators. Presence and Sample One are samplers—they create sounds by shaping short recordings of other instruments and sounds. Impact, the drum machine that you worked with in Chapter Three, is also a sampler. To gain an understanding of the workings of each of Mai Tai, Presence, and Sample One, make sure you watch the videos on this book's online companion. You can also read through the excellent step-by-step descriptions of each of these virtual instruments in Studio One's reference manual by going to Help > Studio One Reference Manual > Built-In Virtual Instruments.

Figure 5-3. Mai Tai's graphical user interface.

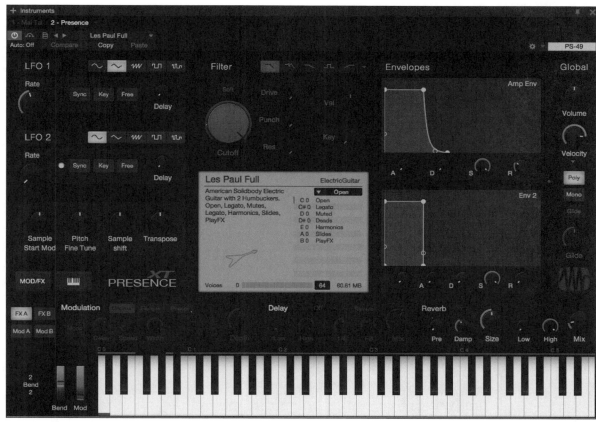

Figure 5-4. Presence's graphical user interface.

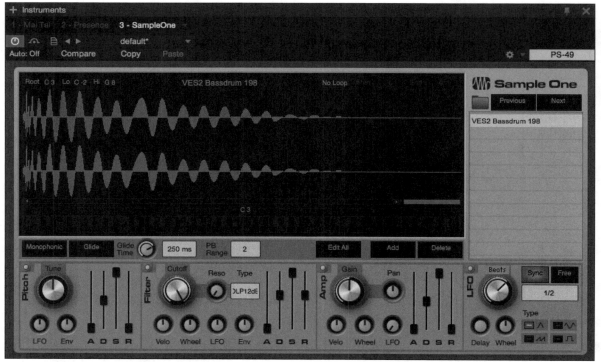

Figure 5-5. Sample One's graphical user interface.

SKILL TEN: LAYERING SOFT SYNTHS TO CREATE A BINARY-FORM COMPOSITION

One of the great things about soft synths is that you can put as many of them as you like into a composition. Fifty years ago, if you wanted to write a piece of music, you were limited to the number of physical instruments you had at your disposal. For example, if you wanted to write music for 12 bassoons, you would need to find 12 bassoon players, each with their own bassoon. With soft synths such as Presence, if you need 12 bassoon sounds, you just create 12 tracks, put Presence on each of them, and dial in a bassoon sound on each track's Presence—you only need one copy of the soft synth, but you can clone it onto as many tracks as you need.

Since we have five virtual instruments in Studio One (Impact, Presence, Mai Tai, Sample One, and Mojito), you might think that we can make music just on five tracks, with one instrument per track, but that's certainly not the case. By using many different versions of Impact, Presence, Mai Tai, Sample One, and Mojito, you can create as many virtual instrument tracks as you like, and you don't have to go out to the music store to buy more instruments.

In this composition, we are going to layer chords with melodies and bass lines to create our music. You already worked with diatonic chords in Chapter Four, but it's fun to go beyond just the diatonic chords in the key. If we stay in C, we can raise the middle note of the iii chord or the vi chord to make III (E, G♯, B) or VI (A, C♯, E), and we can also lower the lowest note of the vii° to make ♭VII (B♭, D, F). All of these chords sound good with other chords in the key of C. Find a piano or electronic keyboard and try moving from I to ♭VII and back—you'll find this in a lot of rock music. Also, try moving from I to III to IV—sounds pretty good, doesn't it?

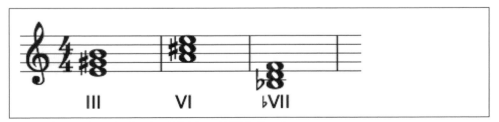

Figure 5-6. Nondiatonic chords of III, VI, and ♭VII in C major.

We can also try writing in a minor mode instead of a major mode. In this case, we would start with A minor (A, C, E) as i, and then use C as III (C, E, G), D minor as iv (D, F, A), E minor as v (E, G, B) or E major as V (E, G♯, B), F as VI (F, A, C), and G as VII (G, B, D).

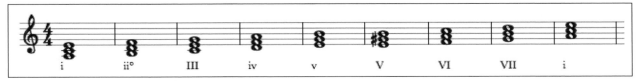

Figure 5-7. Diatonic chords in A minor.

Chords in electronic music work almost like a wash in watercolor painting. It is a surface on which to build your melodies and bass lines. When it comes to finding what chords to put together, and which notes to add to those to create melodies and bass lines, you have two options. One option is to take music theory classes (this usually takes years and is quite challenging). The second option is to improvise, or make it up, until you find sounds you like. Because the computer allows you to listen to your work many times, lets you play with instruments after others have already been recorded, permits you to edit and refine your work, and never runs out of patience, the second option is much more fun and more satisfying. The great American jazz piano player and bandleader Duke Ellington once said, "If it sounds good, it *is* good," and that holds true when you are making your own music. Don't be intimidated by trying to work out if notes are wrong or right—if the notes sound right to you, then the notes *are* right.

Finding the best notes or rhythms to get you started can sometimes feel as strange as pulling a rabbit out of a hat. If it were as easy as the magicians make it look, we would all do it all the time. Of course, there's a trick to the rabbit-out-of-a-hat illusion, as there is with all magical conjurings. Getting started with improvisation is just the same. When great jazz or rock musicians improvise with apparent ease, they are actually working hard at anchoring themselves to patterns and rhythms inside the music. They practice their craft by rehearsing to the same music many times, and the fluidity comes from using licks and riffs that they already know work with the patterns in the music. One excellent thing to do in Studio One is to import Musicloops into the Arrange view as you learned in Skill Two, add a soft synth as you learned in Skill Nine, and then play the soft synth along with the Musicloops. When you have found some musical ideas that you like, record them and then delete the Musicloops tracks.

Listen to a lot of electronic music. You'll find that many composers have created their music in regular patterns of two, four, or eight measures and built up their compositions by layering chords, melodies, and bass lines. Much of the modern approach to composing electronic music was set by groups such as Kraftwerk and Tangerine Dream in the early 1970s, and then expanded by Mike Oldfield, Vangelis, and Jean-Michel Jarre in the later 1970s and into the 1980s. Modern composers, such as Paul van Dyk, Kodomo, Above and Beyond, The M Machine, and Shpongle, have continued this trend of developing electronic music through easily recognizable structures using chords, bass lines, and melody, and they have also included automation of filters and other effects to bring an individuality to electronic music—something that cannot be emulated by other non-electronic musical forms. I have included a list of recommended albums and songs in Chapter Eight. It's a good idea to familiarize yourself with some of these and listen for musical elements in the work as you develop your own compositional skills. You can find almost all of this material on Spotify, iTunes, Apple Music, or YouTube.

We're going to create a song in binary form by layering many soft synth tracks together. *Binary form* means that the song is in two distinct sections; it is sometimes referred to as AB form. Some forms of electronic music, such as dubstep, use binary form regularly—the music builds up through the A section toward a climax or "drop" and then moves into an energetic B section.

1. Open Studio One and create a new song. You can use the blank template. Give your song a random name before you create it. You can always change the name later.

2. Open the Instruments tab in the browser and find the presets for Presence. You may have already discovered some favorite sounds; find a sound you think might be good for playing chords and drag it over into the Arrange view. Improvise and find some chords that will sound good together in a four-measure sequence.

3. Turn the metronome on and click on Record in the transport. Record your chord sequence (remember, you can slow the metronome down if you need to) and click Stop. Open your recorded loop in the Edit view, quantize the notes, and then humanize

them if you wish. Make sure your chord sequence fits exactly into four measures.

4. If necessary, move your recorded chord sequence in the Arrange view so that it starts right at the beginning of the timeline. Select the region you have created and press D seven times to duplicate it. You should have eight repetitions of the region.

5. Find another instrument in Presence that will work well with chords and drag it into the Arrange view under your first track. Select the second repeat of your chord sequence by clicking on it, and then hold the cmd key (ctrl on a PC) as you drag this region down to the new track. It should copy the notes exactly. Now press D six times to repeat that region.

6. Listen to your music so far. You should hear the chord sequence played on one Presence before the second Presence comes in to thicken the texture. You may need to adjust the level of each track to balance them. The best way to do this is by using the Volume rotary dial on each Presence. You can switch between both Presence synths by selecting the numbered tabs at the top of the virtual instrument window. This is a very useful feature when comparing and contrasting synth sounds and settings.

7. Now add a bass sound to the Arrange view by dragging a Mai Tai bass preset onto a new track.

8. As you listen to the chord sequence in your song, find a bass pattern or riff that goes along with it. Begin with notes already in your chords, but feel free to go beyond that to find other combinations. When you are ready, record your new bass part in measures 9–12. Quantize it and edit it so that it fits exactly four measures, and then press D five times.

9. Add another bass track, copy the bass region from measures 13–16 down into it by holding down cmd (ctrl on a PC) and dragging the bass part onto it, and then press D four times.

10. Now listen to your music from the start to this point and make volume adjustments (use the Global Volume control in Mai Tai to adjust volume). You will hear that your music is really now beginning to build as each instrument comes in and adds to the texture.

11. Next, find a melody or lead setting in Mojito and create a fifth track with this sound. Find a melody line to go with your chords and bass so far. Record the melody in measures 17–20, press D

three times. Then add another melody or lead track and copy the melody from measures 21–24 into the new track and press D twice.

12. Listen to your music so far and balance all six instruments using their respective Gain dials.

13. You can probably tell by now that you have two instruments to go. These should be your own choice. Maybe you'd like to add a second melody or some rhythmic chords, or even drums using Impact. Having two Impact kits play the same percussion notes can be quite a cool effect.

14. At this point, you have completed the A section of the music. It should look like a right triangle with the hypotenuse going diagonally down the Arrange view. Save your work.

15. In the B section, you are going to do something very similar, but you are going to keep the exact same eight tracks and therefore the exact same virtual instruments. This time, it is up to you what instrument to start the new section with. You can start with bass, lead, or drums if you wish, or start again with chords. Record four measures of new material, and then edit, duplicate, and copy as before. Build up your music again by adding new ideas in every other four-measure section and thickening it up with another instrument. Remember, though, that you cannot play chords in Mojito, as it is a monophonic synthesizer. Make sure you save your work when you have completed it.

16. When you have completed this skill, you will have a newly composed piece of electronic music in binary form that should be 64 measures long. As you listen to it, you will see how the technique of layering the soft synths together helps the music build and how the composition is linked and has structure because the same instruments are used in both the A and B sections. This is similar to how a composer of orchestral music might build a piece by layering together chords, bass, and melody, and might go through different musical sections in the composition, but ultimately still uses the same instruments to make the music. As you continue to listen to electronic music for ideas, listen to other types of music as well, particularly acoustic instrumental music. You'll start to hear the similarities and connections more than you might think.

BONUS SKILL: TRANSPOSING

One of the great things about composing on a computer is that you can compose in any key you feel comfortable with and then very easily transpose into another key later if you need to. You may prefer to write in C major or A minor because they are relatively simple to find chords in, but then somebody may want to use your music as part of a remix or mash-up, and he will need you to send it to him in a different key so it will work with the other music. Studio One enables you to transpose anything you've already recorded by moving all the notes for you—it's that easy.

1. Work out how many half steps higher or lower you need to move your music. For example, if your music is in C and you wish to transpose it up to F, find C on your PS-49 MIDI Controller and count up the number of half steps it takes to get to F. (The correct number is five.)
2. Holding the Shift button on the computer keyboard, click every region in your music that has notes. Do not select any Impact tracks or other drums; moving these notes will result in different sounds, and you do not want that.
3. From the Event menu, select Musical Functions > Transpose. In the dialog box that opens, use the Add/Subtract option to tell Studio One to transpose your music up by the required number of half steps. To move up from C to F, move the slider to the left to the number 5. If you wanted to transpose down from C to F, you would move the slider to –7.
4. You can use the transpose function to transpose individual regions if you wish, or to transpose portions of a song. As you write a piece of music in a binary or ternary form (see Project E), you could change the key of one of your sections completely to add variety to your music.

STEAM PROBLEM SOLVING: CREATING SOUND WITH ELECTRONICS

Synthesizers are an essential part of Music Technology. They are designed to *synthesize* or re-create the sounds of musical instruments through the manipulation of electronic sounds, and they are capable of creating new sounds never before heard.

Figure 5-8. Professor Léon Theremin playing his invention.

The beginnings of sound synthesis can be traced back to Russian inventor Léon Theremin. Theremin was a professor at the Physical Technical Institute in Petrograd (St. Petersburg), Russia, from 1919 to 1927, where he worked on creating electronic circuits to detect electrical charges in gases. When he added a sound-generating device to one of his circuits, he discovered that he could change the pitch being generated by the device by the position of his hands around the circuit. By altering the magnetic field around the circuit, he was changing the frequency of the sound, and he found that he could play simple melodies just through his proximity to the circuit.

Theremin was a cellist as well as a physicist, so he became intrigued by the possibilities of this new discovery. He modified the circuit and added two antennae, one of which he could use to alter the pitch of the generated sound wave, and one that he could use to change the volume of the sound. Both antennae worked by sensing the proximity of the performer to the instrument's magnetic field, one controlling the frequency of the wave (hence pitch control) and the other the amplitude of the wave (hence volume control). Contemporary audiences were astounded by the instrument because not only did it create new sounds never heard before, but it also worked by the performer waving his arms around it and never actually touching it.

Professor Theremin called this new invention the *Etherwave*.

Theremin moved to New York City in 1927, created his own physics lab and studio in a downtown brownstone building, and developed the Etherwave into a legitimate musical instrument. He patented the device in 1928 and, with the help of the RCA Victor Company, began production of the instrument, first known in the United States as *The Victor Theremin*, and eventually just by the name *Theremin*. Clara Rockmore, a professional New York musician and fellow Russian emigrée, became a virtuoso on the instrument and played many concerts in which she performed classical melodies and concertos on the Theremin.

Figure 5-9. Clara Rockmore playing the Theremin.

The principle of the Theremin is simple. The instrument is capable of generating one continuous sound wave, and the performer shapes the sound by physically manipulating the two main components of the sound wave—frequency and amplitude.

Sound waves move toward the listener by pushing and pulling the air in a process of *compression* and *rarefaction*. The amount of time that it takes one sound wave to compress and then rarefy is one cycle, and the number of cycles completed in one second is the *frequency* of the wave, measured in Hertz (Hz). A sound of less than 20 Hz, or 20 cycles per second, is not easily distinguishable to the human ear as a pitch. Similarly, anything above 20,000 Hz is inaudible to the human ear. Sounds between 20 Hz and 15,000 Hz are easily distinguishable as pitch. Sounds between 15,000 Hz and 20,000 Hz are very difficult to hear, and in fact all humans lose their ability to hear such high frequencies as they get older.

The amount of force with which the sound wave compresses and rarefies is its amplitude, measured in decibels of sound pressure level (dB SPL). Higher sound pressure levels mean louder volume, and anything above 120 dB SPL is uncomfortable for humans to hear. (We refer to 120dB SPL as the "threshold of pain.") Whenever you are exposed to sounds above 120 dB SPL, such as when you are at a rock concert or hear a jet engine or a pneumatic drill, it is important to take time to let your ears recover from that intense sound pressure level. Listening to sounds around and above 120 dB SPL for long periods of time can cause permanent hearing damage.

Another New Yorker, Robert Moog, took Theremin's invention to the next level and added many features to refine and control the sound. Moog is widely regarded as the inventor of the modern-day synthesizer. Robert Moog originally started his own electronics company to create and sell Theremins, but he soon began to develop his own Moog line of musical instruments. Moog used an electronic device called an *audio oscillator* to generate sound. By combining more than one oscillator, he was able to alter the quality of the sound produced and affect the shape of the sound wave. He controlled the oscillators by electrical voltage and added a piano keyboard–like controller to dictate what voltage the oscillators produced. By doing this, a performer could now dictate pitch precisely. Moog added low-frequency oscillators (oscillating below 20 Hz) to modulate the sound through vibrato, tremolo, panning, and so on and also added envelope circuits that were able to control the passage of the sound through the amplifier section of the synthesizer, controlling its attack, decay, sustain, and release phases. Moog's developments are the basis of all modern sound synthesis techniques, and you can probably recognize many of his ideas in the controls you see in Studio One's Presence, Mai Tai, and Mojito.

Figure 5-10. Robert Moog with a Moog synthesizer.

PROJECT E: COMPOSING ELECTRONIC MUSIC IN TERNARY FORM

As you worked through Chapter Five, you created a piece of music in binary, or AB, form. In this project, you will extend your skills of creating melodies, bass lines, and chord sequences with soft synths to compose a piece of music in ternary, or ABA, form.

Repetition is vital in music. Listeners enjoy coming back to music they have heard before, so in ternary form, you repeat the first section after the second section. When you return to the first section, you can alter it if you wish, maybe by adding more instruments and rhythms, but it should still be recognizable as the first section repeated.

HELPFUL TIPS

- Write your music in sections that adhere to powers of 2 in length—4, 8, 16, 32, and so on.

- If you use mostly the same instruments in each section, your music will sound unified, even if the chords, melodies, and bass lines change.
- Remember that you can create your own Musicloops in Studio One and draw from this pool of loops in your composing work. As you create new ideas, you should export these to the "My Musicloops" folder you created in Chapter Three. Most professional producers and composers compile extensive libraries of their own loops, which they can then choose from as they create new compositions.
- You should not give your listeners an impression that each section is a new song. Listen carefully to how the music moves from one section to the next, and avoid large moments of silence.
- Structure is very important to music. When professional producers write beats or other electronic music, they are often working through simple, pre-organized forms.
- If you're feeling ambitious, you can extend ternary form by adding more musical ideas. Rondo form (a term we borrow from the poetic term *rondeau*) adds more sections, called episodes, but always returns to A after each. It would be represented ABACA or ABACADA, perhaps. Extended ternary form nests three ternary-form sections within one ternary-form piece of music! It's easier to think of it as ABA CDC ABA.
- Every time you return to an A section, you can decorate or embellish it by adding more musical elements, but you should never disguise the music so much that it is unrecognizable from the original A section.

PROJECT REQUIREMENTS CHECKLIST

Your project should include

- An A section of at least eight measures.
- A B section of at least eight measures.
- A final section that returns to the original A section, with added decoration and embellishment.
- At least three virtual instruments used in the music: Impact, Mojito, Mai Tai, Presence, and/or Sample One.
- A written summary of your challenges and successes in completing this project.

RECORDING AND EDITING IN STUDIO ONE 6

CHAPTER SIX GOAL AND OBJECTIVES

The goal of this chapter is to familiarize you with recording in Studio One through the Audiobox USB interface. As you read and work through the chapter, you will

- Record external instruments, sounds, and/or voices.
- Use Studio One's editing tools.
- Add effects to an audio track.
- Use Ampire, Studio One's amp modeling plug-in.
- Compose and layer motifs to create a composition.
- Create an idea for a new video game, with appropriate music.
- Trace the history of recording and the important contributions of Thomas Edison, Emile Berliner, Fritz Pfluemer, and Les Paul.

INTRODUCTION

In Chapter Five, we learned how to record music in Studio One via virtual instruments, or soft synths, using the PS-49 MIDI Controller. In this chapter, we are going to explore recording external instruments, such as voice, electric guitar, and bass guitar, using the Audiobox USB audio interface. Check that your interface is connected to your computer and also make sure you are using the powered USB hub provided with the PreSonus *Music Creation Suite*.

SKILL ELEVEN: RECORDING VOCALS, ELECTRIC GUITARS, BASSES, AND OTHER INSTRUMENTS

1. Open Studio One and create a new song. Use the Audiobox USB template (not the Audiobox USB Stereo template).
2. You will notice that Studio One gives you two tracks, both in Record Ready mode, labeled **Input L** and **Input R**. These correspond to Inputs 1 and 2 on the front of the Audiobox. You can

change what track is recording what input just by clicking on the Input Label on the track header. The red light on each track header shows that the track is ready to record, and the blue light shows that you are able to monitor the incoming signal through your headphones. Turn both the Gain dials on the front of the Audiobox all the way to the left. Turn the Mixer dial to Inputs. Make sure your Phones level is not too loud.

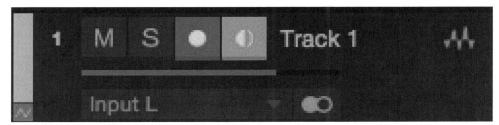

Figure 6-1. Track header, showing track ready to record and monitoring input.

3. Connect your microphone to Input 1, turn on the 48V phantom power, and speak into your microphone (or play an acoustic musical instrument) at a normal level while turning the Gain dial for Input 1 to the right. As you begin to turn the dial, you should see signal coming into Track 1 in Studio One and hear it through your headphones. Keep turning the dial until you get a strong signal without lighting the clip light on the front of the Audiobox (the track level indicator in Studio One will also turn red). If you do raise the Gain past the point of clipping, turn it back again by a few degrees and reset the track level indicator in Track 1 by clicking it with the mouse.

4. Now record the sound you just used to test the recording level. If you wish to record to a click track, use the metronome at the bottom of the screen. You can set the tempo of the metronome by adjusting the tempo indication. There are three icons in the metronome panel. The rightmost icon turns the metronome on and off, the middle icon allows you to change the metronome properties, and the leftmost icon tells Studio One to give you a count-off in clicks before recording. Click on the Record button in the transport and sing, speak, or play your instrument. When you have finished, click Stop and then Return-to-Zero. If you want to listen to your recording, move the Mixer dial back toward Playback and click on Play.

Figure 6-2. The metronome panel in Studio One.

5. Now look at the editing tools at the top of the Studio One Arrange view. Each of these can be accessed quickly by using the number keys as shortcuts.

- Number 1 is the Arrow tool. With this selected, you can edit the front and end of a region when you hover the mouse and drag horizontally from the beginning or end of the section you recorded. You can also fade in or fade out audio clips by hovering and dragging diagonally from the top-left or right corner, and you can alter the overall volume of the region by hovering and dragging up or down right in the top middle of the clip.
- Number 2 is the Range tool, which allows you to select a portion of the audio recording, much like selecting text in a word processor. Try selecting just part of the audio and then hitting the delete key (make sure you use the Undo feature afterward).
- The Split tool (number 3) allows you to slice your region, so you can move parts of it around precisely.
- The Eraser tool (number 4) lets you delete any section by clicking on it.
- The Paint tool (number 5) is used for drawing automation; we will look at this tool in more detail in Chapter Seven.
- The Mute tool (number 6) is a quick way to mute sections of a song or recording.
- The Bend tool (number 7) allows you to move small sections of the audio within a region; this is useful if you have drum hits or chords that are not quite on the beat and need to be aligned.
- The Listen tool (number 8) allows you to audition any part of the recording just by clicking on the audio and holding the mouse button down.

Figure 6-3. Studio One's editing tools.

6. Open the browser, click on the Effects tab, and open the PreSonus folder. Here, you will find all the audio effects that come bundled with Studio One. Each effect has many presets, and you can apply any of these presets to the sound you have recorded just by dragging and dropping any of them from the browser to the track you recorded on. As you drop the preset on the track, you will see the effect drawn on the screen, similarly to the virtual instruments that we worked with in Chapter Five. These effects are again virtual, and you can edit any parameters of the effects to alter the sound. Listen to your recording after you've added some effects, and try altering the parameters in the virtual device. Listening and experimenting is a great way to learn what these effects do. A full explanation of them all would require a second volume of this book, but we will learn specifically about the Compressor, Pro EQ, Channel Strip, and Limiter in Chapter Seven.

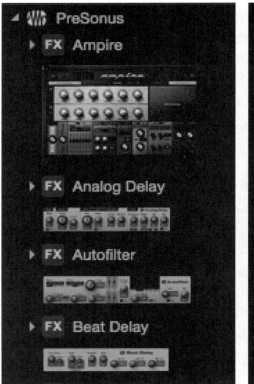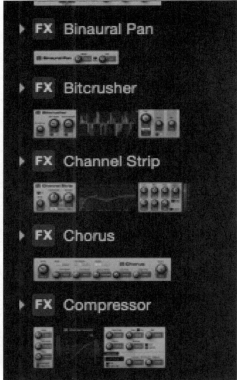

Figure 6-4. Some of Studio One's audio effects, as shown in the browser.

7. Open the Mix view and find the channel strip for the track you recorded on. Click on the right-pointing arrow to bring up the track's extended view, and you will see the Inserts pane for the track. Here, you can reorder any insert's effects by clicking and

moving them up or down, turn them off by clicking the blue Power icon by the insert effect's name, or remove them by using ctrl-click (right-click on a PC). You can also open a smaller, graphical version of the effect in the mixer by using cmd-click (ctrl-click on a PC).

8. Take time to experiment with the effects in Studio One. They truly are some of the best you will find in any Digital Audio Workstation, and the drag-and-drop functionality makes them easy and fun to use. Almost any time you add a PreSonus effect to a track in Studio One, the recording sounds better in some way. You can find out more about the included effects in the Studio One Reference Manual, which you can find in the Help menu.

9. Try recording different acoustic instruments in Studio One by using the microphone. Also try adding different effects to the recordings you make. Always make sure to place the microphone close to the sound that you are recording, preferably between three and six inches from the instrument. The microphone cable supplied with the PreSonus *Music Creation Suite* is quite long and should allow you to move the microphone closer to whatever it is you're recording. Do watch out, though, that you don't accidentally drag your audio interface or computer onto the floor! If you need more cable length, you can always buy another XLR cable at any electronics store and connect the cables together to cover more ground.

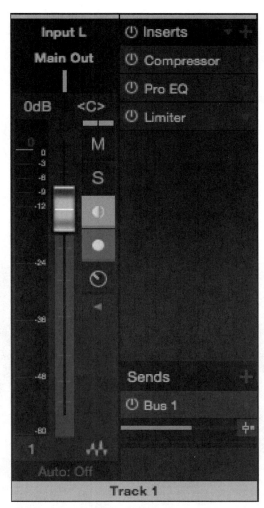

Figure 6-5. Extended Channel Strip view in the mixer, showing Inserts and Sends.

10. If you wish to record electric guitar or bass guitar, connect a 1/4-inch guitar cable from the instrument to one of the inputs on the front of the Audiobox. As usual, turn the Gain dial for that channel all the way left before connecting, and then turn the dial to the right as you play the instrument until you get a strong signal without clipping. You do not need 48V phantom power for recording electric guitar or bass.

11. Studio One contains a virtual guitar amp for guitar and bass, called Ampire. Look for it in the PreSonus folder within the Effects tab of the browser. You can insert Ampire onto the guitar or bass track and adjust the type of amp and cabinet that the guitar or bass plays through. If you click the button labeled **Stomps**, you can also add various foot pedals to your sound. Note that when you record guitar, you are recording the unprocessed signal, and Ampire is added to the sound as it plays back. That way, you can change the sound of the guitar even after it has already been recorded.

Figure 6-6. Ampire, showing the Stomps.

12. In Studio One, you can record on two tracks at once if you like. That way, if you're playing electric guitar and singing along, you can record both parts at the same time. Just make sure you have your microphone and a guitar connected to the two inputs at the front of the Audiobox USB and that both tracks are Record Ready when you record. You will need the 48V phantom power to be on if you are recording using the PreSonus M7 microphone or another condenser microphone, but this will not cause damage to an instrument connected to the other channel.

SKILL TWELVE: COMPOSING VIDEO GAME MUSIC BY LAYERING MOTIFS

Imagine that you have been contacted by a video game company. They would like you to share your ideas for a brand new video game. You will need to design and create a series of scenes, levels, or worlds, and you will present these ideas to them with accompanying music that illustrates and enhances every different part of the game. To create unity among all the levels in your video game music, we are going to borrow a compositional technique from trance and ambient music, and then we will learn how to create alternate mixes of our composed work as we continue into Chapter Seven.

Some of the albums mentioned in Chapter Eight are fine examples of trance and ambient music. Listen especially to albums by Jean-Michel Jarre, Kodomo, and Shpongle, and you will see how the artists achieve ebb and flow in their music by adding new ideas and fading out old ones as the music progresses. A track such as "Dorset Perception," from Shpongle's *Tales of the Inexpressible*, illustrates this very clearly. From the beginning of the song, new musical material is added every four measures by way of a new instrument, a new rhythm, a new chord progression, a new bass line, and so on. As the song progresses, you begin to realize that musical ideas you heard earlier have somehow disappeared in the texture, but sometimes they return as the music continues.

In Chapter Eight, you will also find some examples of excellent video game soundtracks. Search for some of these on Spotify, Apple Music, or YouTube and listen to them. You will notice that the music is often continuous, moving seamlessly between contrasting passages of music, allowing the gameplay to be uninterrupted while still adding atmosphere and excitement to the game-playing experience. The speed of the music is often directly related to the atmosphere of the game—racing and platform games tend to have fast soundtracks, mystery and relaxation games tend to have slower soundtracks. The technique of keeping the music flowing is often exactly the same technique used in creating ambient and trance music, and it involves the layering and fading out of short musical phrases that we call *motifs*.

1. Choose a theme for a video game. Later on, you will be able to work out the details, but for now just start with a basic idea of what you would want your game to be.
2. Create a new song in Studio One and choose the Audiobox USB template. If your game is going to be fast and exciting, choose a tempo between 95 and 140 bpm; if your game is going to be slow and relaxing, choose a tempo between 60 and 95 bpm. You can always change the tempo later if you wish.
3. Decide how you want your music to start. You could begin by using a beat that you make in Impact, creating something in a soft synth, or recording an acoustic instrument or electric guitar. If you do decide to use a soft synth, drag a preset into the Arrange view from the browser. If you decide to use an acoustic instrument or an electric guitar, make sure you have made the right connections to the Audiobox USB and that you have set a good recording level.
4. The first music you need to create should be four measures long. Enable the metronome, click Play on the transport, and improvise until you find something cool to record. Then record your music into Studio One and edit it so it is exactly four measures long. Place it at the start of the song and press the letter D on the computer keyboard three times to loop that measure out to 16 measures. Create a fade-out in the last few measures. In ambient and trance music, these short phrases are known as *motifs*. Because motifs are short and repetitive, you can add other motifs to them as long as you can find ideas that work well together— you do not need to worry too much about harmonic progressions or building of tension and release in the music because you are keeping the listener at the same level of excitement or relaxation throughout the music. It is very important, however, to be meticulous about quantizing beats and soft synth motifs and editing any recordings precisely.

5. Choose a different instrument and work out another motif to go along with what you just recorded. You can use the loop brace to play your first motif over and over again as you improvise a new musical idea. When you are ready, record the new motif and edit it so it fits in measures 5–9. Press the letter D to loop it out to measure 20, and create a fade-out in the last few measures.

6. Add two more motifs this way, one fitting in measures 9–24 and one in measures 13–28. If you need to add another track for recording through the Audiobox USB, select Add Audio Track (mono) from the Track menu. You can also use the shortcut letter T or double-click in the blank space under the track headers to bring up the Add Track dialog.

7. At measure 29, you have a choice to make. You could add a fifth motif to the music on a new track, you could layer the first motif out for another 16 measures, or you could record a new motif using the instrument you used for the first idea. Whatever you choose to do, you should again create four measures duplicated three times for a total of 16 measures.

8. Listen to your music continually as you progress to see if you should add new ideas or bring back ideas you've used before. As your music begins to move from one idea to another, you will hear how it is beginning to ebb and flow just like trance or ambient music. Keep going until you have 40–60 measures of music. Save your work.

9. One thing you may like to do during this project is to create some four-measure motifs in Notion and export them individually as audio files to add into Studio One. This can be very useful if you are the sort of composer who benefits from seeing the notes on the screen in standard notation rather than composing by recording and quantizing. Remember to set the tempo of your Notion file to be the same as the tempo of your Studio One file so that the exported motifs are at the correct speed for the rest of the project.

10. As you compose, let the music suggest to you how the game itself will progress—what the story will be, what worlds or levels the game will go through, who the characters will be, what skills or artifacts they will need to pick up through the game, how the game will end, and so on.

11. Write down some notes about the game on paper or maybe make some visual sketches of the gameplay. You will need this when you get to Project G.

BONUS SKILL: EXPORTING FROM STUDIO ONE

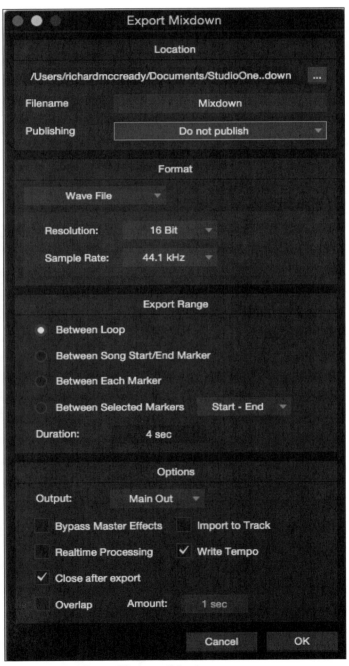

Figure 6-7. The Export Mixdown dialog box.

1. Open your video game composition in Studio One.

2. In the Arrange view, use the loop brace at the top left of the timeline to specify the beginning and end of your song.

3. Choose Export Mixdown from the Song menu and select the option to export Between Loop. In the top box of the Export Mixdown dialog, choose a place to save the mixdown and a name for your exported song. Leave the format as Wave File (.wav) and click OK to perform the mixdown.

4. This .wav file can now be exported into other projects or added to media players such as iTunes or Windows Media Player. You can even put it on your iPod or smartphone to listen to on the go.

   WAV files are quite large; if you want to export to the smaller compressed MP3 format instead, you can purchase the Studio One MP3 Converter for $10 from the PreSonus website (https://shop.presonus.com/products/studio-one-prods/studio-one-add-ons).

5. The Export Mixdown option also allows you to publish your song to Nimbit. Nimbit is a music publishing service that is free when you buy the PreSonus *Music Creation Suite.* Simply go to http://nimbit.com to set up your own account, and you will be able to direct friends and family there to listen to or download your music.

STEAM PROBLEM SOLVING: RECORDING AND OVERDUBBING

The history of audio recording begins in the 1870s, when Thomas Edison invented the *phonograph.* The phonograph was capable of both recording and playing back sound. The process is quite simple. A microphone diaphragm transmits the vibration of sound waves to a cutting *stylus* that etches a groove into a tinfoil cylinder. The picture of the sound waves created on the cylinder is *analogous* to the sound, from which we get the term *analog.* After the cylinder has been cut, the phonograph can then play the sound back by using the stylus to relay the sound waves to another moving diaphragm—this time a speaker. (In fact, a microphone and a speaker do exactly the same job, but in opposite directions; a microphone translates sound vibration into an analog or digital signal, and a speaker converts an analog or digital signal into sound vibrations.)

Emile Berliner created a similar device that he called the *gramophone.* The principle was the same as Edison's phonograph but used shellac platters instead; they eventually became known as records.

Figure 6-8. Thomas Edison with his phonograph.

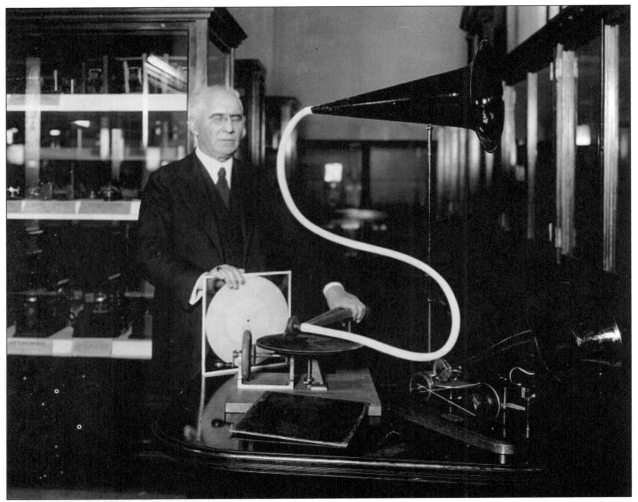

Figure 6-9. Emile Berliner with his gramophone.

The biggest problem with both the phonograph and the gramophone was that if you made a mistake in cutting the cylinder or record, there was no way to undo the damage. You just had to dispose of the cylinder or record you had been cutting. Musicians had to record their music in one take only, and there was certainly no room for error. If you made a mistake on the recording, most of the time you just had to live with it.

Fritz Pfluemer developed a new recording medium in the late 1920s—recording tape. Recording tape is magnetic. As you record onto it, a tape machine arranges the magnetic filings on the tape in a pattern analogous to the sound waves. Instead of a single stylus, the tape machine has two *heads*, a record head and a play head. When you press the Record button on the machine, the record head magnetizes the tape, and when you press Play, the play head reads the magnetic pattern and passes that on to the speaker. Because of the two separate heads, if you record something and need a do-over, you just rewind the tape and re-record over the recording you just made. That completely erases the first recording as you create the second one.

Recording tape is also very versatile in that you can edit it by cutting it and splicing it back together again. That way, if you wish to re-record just one small part of a song, you do not have to redo the entire recording. You can record just the small section you need to replace onto a different piece of tape and then insert it in the appropriate place on the first recording.

Interestingly, the tape machine was used for espionage by the Germans during the Second World War; they recorded conversations and radio broadcasts when they spied on the countries they were at war with. After the war was over, the victorious Allies seized on this new invention and brought it back to their own countries, where it would be used for a much better purpose—to record music. One of the Americans who was over in Europe at the end of the war and witnessed this new technology firsthand was the singer and movie star Bing Crosby, who regularly travelled to the war front to entertain U.S. troops. After the war, he invested $50,000 in a new company called Ampex that built the first American tape machines.

One of the members of Bing Crosby's band at the time was a young musician named Les Paul, who was one of the

Figure 6-10. An Ampex reel-to-reel tape machine.

finest jazz guitar players in the country. As well as being a superb guitarist, Les Paul loved to tinker with machines and invent new gadgets. (Les is a member of the Inventors Hall of Fame as well as being in the Rock and Roll Hall of Fame, the Jazz Hall of Fame, the Big Band Hall of Fame, the Grammy Hall of Fame, and the Songwriters Hall of Fame.)

Bing gave Les a new portable Ampex tape machine so that he could record duets with his wife, Mary Ford, when they were on tour together. As soon as Les started to work with this new device, he noticed that the record head was positioned before the play head as the tape passed through the mechanism, and wondered if an alternative placement could result in the tape machine recording something at the same time as playing something else. Les telephoned the Ampex company, ordered another record head, and installed it beside the play head on his machine. He discovered that he was able to record himself playing the guitar, and then record a second guitar track on top of the first one. The tape machine was playing one track via the play head and recording another via the second record head. What Les had invented was called *sound on sound* or *overdubbing*. For the first time, people would be able to commit multiple recordings of themselves onto the same piece of tape. This was a major

Figure 6-11. Les Paul with his eight-track Ampex tape machine.

breakthrough in recording history that gave way to modern Music Technology techniques that allow us to build up a composition by layering many sounds on top of one another. Les and his wife made many recordings together as Les Paul and Mary Ford, and some of those recordings feature as many as twelve guitars (all played by Les) and twelve vocal parts (all sung by Mary), all recorded on that original Ampex tape machine.

It is certainly worth suggesting that Les and Mary also created the world's first portable home studio, as they took that same tape machine on all their travels and recorded in different halls, hotels, and private homes throughout the United States.

Les Paul's contribution to Music Technology is unquestionable. Without his invention of overdubbing, the whole world of recording would be very different today. Les is also important for pioneering the solidbody electric guitar in conjunction with the Gibson company, which still makes its Les Paul signature model to the same basic specifications that Les created in the 1950s. Les Paul also invented many of the recording techniques we use today, such as reverb and delay. All studio musicians and engineers would agree that not a day goes by in the recording industry that they don't use an invention or technique made possible by Les Paul.

PROJECT F: COMPOSING MUSIC FOR YOUR OWN VIDEO GAME

Earlier in this chapter, we discussed the use of motifs to create music and began the process of writing music suitable for a video game. In this project, your task is to create your basic musical theme for the game and begin to articulate how the game would be designed and how your music illustrates and accompanies the gameplay. You will continue to develop this music and game idea as you work through Chapter Seven and Project G.

HELPFUL TIPS

- Take time over each motif. Make sure that everything you record goes well with other motifs and that you edit and/or quantize after you record.
- Keep listening to electronic music and video game music whenever you're not actively composing. You might hear some ideas that you could translate into your own music.

- Remember to fade out motifs toward the end of their 16 measures. They should disappear into the background imperceptibly. This means that the fade may need to be quite long to be subtle enough.
- If you are continuing a motif for another 16 measures, do not fade it out.
- Experiment with effects as you compose. You can come across some cool ideas quite by accident sometimes.

PROJECT REQUIREMENTS CHECKLIST

Your project should include

- Between 60 and 90 measures of music.
- Four-measure motifs that repeat three times, for a total of 16 measures each.
- Subtle fading at the end of each motif.
- Accurate and appropriate quantizing and editing.
- A written explanation of your basic ideas for your game.
- A written summary of your challenges and successes in completing this project.

MIXING AND MASTERING IN STUDIO ONE

7

CHAPTER SEVEN GOAL AND OBJECTIVES

The goal of this chapter is to familiarize you with the processes of mixing and mastering. As you read and work through the chapter, you will

- Pan each track in a mix appropriately and add pan automation.
- Add a compressor and EQ to each track.
- Adjust the parameters of compression and EQ.
- Experiment with Studio One's Channel Strip Effect.
- Apply compression and EQ to a master track.
- Use limiters in a master track.
- Read about Tom Dowd and the development of modern mixing desks.
- Create a PowerPoint or Keynote presentation of your video game music and ideas.

INTRODUCTION

In this chapter, we are going to use the music that you created for your video game to create alternative mixes. By doing this, we will be able to experiment with mixing and mastering plug-ins within Studio One and also create different versions of your music, which you can then use as part of a final project that shows the developing layers and worlds in your video game.

SKILL THIRTEEN: ADDING PLUG-IN EFFECTS AND AUTOMATION

1. Open the video game music you created in Chapter Six and use the File > Save As command to save multiple versions of your song. Give each a unique name. For example, if your song was called My Game, save multiple versions as My Game 1, My Game 2, My Game 3, and so on.

2. Open the original version and listen to it all the way through to familiarize yourself with it again. As you listen, think about the balance among the tracks, how some elements might need to be boosted or cut in the mix, and how some sounds might benefit from being panned left or right in the headphones.

3. Open the Mix view. As you listen to the music, decide where sounds should be in the left-right audio spectrum. Use the pan slider on each track's fader strip to move sounds left or right in the mix. Moving sounds into different places will help clarify the mix. No two sounds should occupy the same vertical space, or one will mask the other, just as one actor standing in front of another on stage will cause the other actor to be obscured from view.

4. You may wish to automate panning on a track, to make a sound move from one side to another while the music plays (this is a very cool effect). Ctrl-click (right-click on a PC) on the pan slider and select Edit Pan Automation. You will now see an extra track added to the Arrange view. Use the Paint tool (Edit tool number 5) to draw automation on the vertical line through the new track. The position of the vertical line up or down affects the position of the track in the audio spectrum—moving the line up moves the sound to the left, and moving the line down moves the sound to the right. You can change the Paint tool by clicking the small triangle at the bottom right of the icon. Listen to the music again and you will see the pan slider move all by itself in the Mix view!

5. After completing the panning phase of mixing, you need to work on dynamics, or the loudness and softness of each track. Believe it or not, the volume faders in the Mix view are the last things you should use to control volume in a professional mix. Instead, you should use the Compressor and the Pro EQ plug-in effects to control the dynamics of each track.

   Solo the first track in your song. Find the Compressor plug-in within the PreSonus folder in the Effects tab of the browser. Drag the compressor over the track, either in the Arrange view or the Mix view, and you will see the virtual graphical interface. The compressor has a lot of presets that you can try, or you can alter the parameters yourself. The idea of the compressor is to level out the dynamics in your track by boosting the quieter volumes without boosting the louder volumes too much. You should use a ratio of between 2.0:1 and 4.0:1 for the most realistic results. As you raise the ratio, you will see that the top of the graph bands down, thereby lowering the upper volumes. As you bring the threshold up, the amount of sounds squeezed at the top end increases. The Knee parameter controls how angular the dip is at the threshold. Finally, the Gain setting allows you to boost the overall output of the compressor.

Obviously you do not want the track to clip, so you need to be careful. Studio One's compressor includes an Auto Gain function that you can use if you wish. Attack and Release control how fast the compressor works—you should lengthen the attack if you want a percussive start to each sound, or shorten it if you want a smoother start. Similarly, you should reduce the release time if you want a sharp cutoff to each note, or lengthen it if you want the sound to tail off more smoothly.

You can automate any of the parameters in the compressor by using the same method as automating the panning—ctrl-click (right-click on a PC) the parameter you wish to automate, and a new track will open for it in the Arrange view. You may wish to lower the Gain of each track as new motifs appear in the music.

Figure 7-1. Studio One's Compressor plug-in.

6. Listen to each track in solo mode and then without solo mode as you add a compressor to each track. Be ready to go back and

adjust any compressors you added earlier or to adjust panning if necessary.

7. Solo the first track in your song again. Add the Pro EQ from the PreSonus effects. Again, you can choose from several presets or alter the parameters yourself. The Pro EQ shows you the frequencies of sound from 20 Hz to 20,000 Hz and allows you to adjust the sound produced by the track by boosting or cutting these frequencies. The Pro EQ has seven bands you can adjust: Low Cut, Low, Low Medium, Medium, High Medium, High, and High Cut. Each band corresponds to a colored dot that you can move around in the EQ either by using the rotary dials or by

Figure 7-2. Studio One's Pro EQ plug-in.

dragging the dots in the graph. The Q in each band refers to the width of the point you are boosting or cutting. Be aware that as you boost parts of the sound, you are increasing the volume, and as you cut sounds, you are lowering the volume. You can use the Gain dial in the EQ to compensate for this.

8. Listen to each track in your song in solo mode and without solo mode and add a Pro EQ to each track. As you work, you may need to return to earlier choices you made in panning and compression and readjust. Being willing to make changes to work you have already done is a major part of the mixing process.

9. Click on the right-pointing triangle in each Mix view track to check the order of the inserts on each track. When you work with electronic music, it is best to have any effects—such as reverb, chorus, flanger, and so on—at the top of the chain, followed by the compressor and finally the Pro EQ. Some engineers prefer to put the compressor after the EQ, particularly when working with the soft sounds found in atmospheric or some classical music, but it is a matter of personal choice.

10. Remember that you can automate anything in the mix. Each automation track has a green Automation Mode button labeled **Read** when you first apply the automation. You can set this to Auto:Off if you wish to bypass the automation you have created. You can also use Write mode to create the automation by moving the parameters while the track plays. (Always remember not to use Record to do this—you do not record automation, you write it.) After using Write mode, remember to return the track to Read mode again. You can also use the Touch or Latch modes to perform some fine-tuning of the written automation, though it is (quite honestly) easier just to use the Paint tool.

11. Save this new version of your mix. Now open another unmixed version and try creating a different mix. You can try altering the speed of your music or adding different panning, compression, and EQ settings. You could alter the priority of the relative volumes of each instrument—something that was a background sound in one mix may become a foreground sound in another. It can often be fun to add more instruments and drums as you mix, even to create a remix of your own mix! It is best to do this from an unmixed version, or choices you made in a different

mix could unfairly alter the final output, making all your mixes sound too similar.

12. Another option for compression and EQ is the Channel Strip Effect—it is a plug-in that combines both compression and EQ parameters into one interface. As you develop your mixing skills, try using it instead of the compressor/EQ combination.

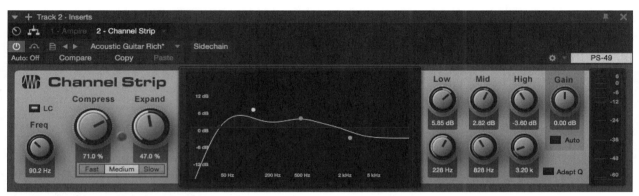

Figure 7-3. Studio One's Channel Strip plug-in.

13. As you create new mixes and remixes of your music, think of what scenes, levels, or worlds these might be good for in your game. Ultimately, you are creating multiple variations of the same musical material so that people playing your game always feel they are in the same game, because the music is similar, without getting bored hearing the same thing over and over again.

14. A good way to provide variety between mixes is to add different beats to the music. You can do this by using the Impact virtual instruments or by using Musicloops. When you do this, you have to make sure you create room for your new beats in your EQ settings in the other tracks. You are probably going to want to add bass-heavy beats, in which case you need to cut bass in other tracks so the sounds do not interfere with each other and clog the mix. Whenever you augment a song with extra sounds, you always have to mix it again to compensate for the new material—hence the term *remixing*.

SKILL FOURTEEN: FINAL MIXING AND MASTERING

Mastering is an essential part of the whole process of recording and mixing, and it is often the most difficult and painstaking part to do well. Most artists take their material to someone else to master, and the benefit of having another pair of ears listen to the music is not to be underestimated. With the Artist version of Studio One that is included in the PreSonus *Music Creation Suite*, you are able to do some basic mastering by balancing the tracks one last time and adding polish to the master track. But if you eventually upgrade to the Professional edition of Studio One, you will have access to the entire PreSonus Mastering Suite, which is comprehensive and excellent. More details of the various editions of Studio One can be found at the PreSonus website (http://studioone.presonus.com/compare-versions).

When you master your music, let other people take a listen and give you suggestions. They will often hear things that you may have missed. Also try different headphones and monitor speakers if you have access to them. You should also burn your mixes to CD or put them on your MP3 player and listen to them in different places and on different stereo systems. One of the most important places to listen to a mix is in the car. The road noise masks the mid-range of the music, and you can always rely on the car test to expose problems in the lower and higher ranges that you might not notice otherwise. Always be ready to redo a mix as you gather information from each listening experience, especially as you are learning (and, by the way, the world's best mixers are always learning).

1. Open any of the mixes you created in Skill Thirteen.
2. Listen to the mix again and use the Mix view faders to make any subtle changes in the relative volume of each track. Automate these if you wish to add fade-ins or fade-outs, but be very subtle in your use of them. Never let any track clip.
3. To the far right of the Mix view, you will see the master track, labeled **Main Out**. Insert a compressor on the track and try some presets or adjust parameters to add polish to the sound. If you want to automate any of these parameters, you can do so in the same way as on any other track. Be subtle with your compressor—you want to make sure quieter sounds are heard without overloading the full mix.
4. Add a Pro EQ to the master track and alter the EQ of the sound. Listen intently as you boost and cut certain frequencies to see where the music gets more energy and sparkle and where you can reduce any dullness.

5. If you wish to add any other effects to the master track, insert them before the compressor. You can move effects in the master effect chain by clicking on the right-pointing triangle to open the Extended Channel Strip view and then dragging effects up or down in the list. Some light reverb or delay might lend some atmosphere to your music; some gentle modulation, such as chorus, flanger, or phaser, may also give it a unique flavor. Be very subtle with your use of effects. The rule of thumb with master effects is that if you dial it in so much that a listener can tell what the effect is, you have dialed in too much. Again, another pair of ears will help you.

6. Automate the master fader if you want to fade your whole song in or out. Again, be subtle—slow fades are better than fast ones in the mastering process.

7. The final stage of mastering is the limiter. Find the Limiter plug-in within the PreSonus folder in the browser's effects and add it to the master effects chain below the Pro EQ. The limiter has several presets for boosting the volume level of the master track without clipping. The limiter should never be used to make up for lazy mixing or to compensate for bad compressor and EQ levels, but it is a very useful last stage in the process for giving your music a sonic fullness without introducing distortion.

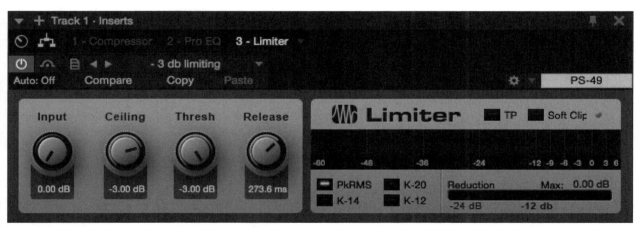

Figure 7-4. Studio One's Limiter plug-in.

8. Save each mix as you complete the mastering process and then apply the same skills to each mix that you created in Skill Thirteen. Try burning all mixes to a CD or putting them on an MP3 player and then listening to them in consecutive and random

order to see if there are any glaring differences in volume or EQ. Be ready to go back and correct any errors you hear.

9. You cannot rush this process. Professionals sometimes take many days to master an album, even though the music has already been recorded and mixed very well. Good mastering can often mean the difference between a song being a hit or a flop, in that the impression people get on first hearing a song is crucial to their potential for liking it, no matter whether they hear it on their car radio, their TV, in the background music at the grocery store, in a movie, in a game, at the doctor's office, at the car showroom, or in any number of places where music can be heard. If the music sparkles with energy and it sounds consistent no matter what sound system or speakers it is played on, then it has every chance of success.

BONUS SKILL: USING BUSES AND SENDS IN STUDIO ONE

If you have several similar tracks that you could combine and send to the same effects plug-in, you can simplify your mix by busing them together or sending them to the same effects channel. Busing works just like putting several people on a bus to move them from place to place, except that we move audio from place to place instead.

1. Hold Shift and click on several tracks to select them together, and then choose Add Bus for Selected Tracks from the Track menu. A new bus track will open, and you can place effects onto this track just as you would any other track. All the tracks that you added to the bus will pass through the same effects; this allows you to control and shape their sounds at the same time.

2. When you use buses, 100 percent of the signal on the track is sent to the chosen effects on the bus. This is very useful when mixing drums or any other instrument that you have recorded with multiple microphones or inputs. If you have recorded guitar and vocals together, it is a very good idea to bus them together with a reverb effect because different levels of reverb in each track gives the impression that they were recorded in separate places.

3. Sends allow you to specify how much of the audio track is sent to an effect. It is similar to busing in its usefulness but slightly

different in its execution. Select any of the tracks you wish to send to an effect unit and expand its Mix view strip by clicking the right-pointing arrow. Click the + icon at the top of the Sends section and add an FX channel. You can add any of the PreSonus effects, including compressor and Pro EQ, to this track. You control the amount of signal you send to the FX channel with the horizontal fade strip in the Sends view. You can send other tracks to the same FX channel by clicking the + icon in their Mix view strips and selecting FX 1 as their destination. You can send any track to more than one FX channel if you wish.

STEAM PROBLEM SOLVING: THE MIXING DESK

Les Paul's invention of sound on sound not only made multitrack recording possible; it also made multitrack mixing possible. As artists began to record their songs on four, six, or eight tracks, it became necessary to find a way to alter the balance and EQ of those tracks simultaneously. The first mixing consoles employed large rotary knobs for controlling volume, treble response, bass response, and so on, but the job of mixing the tracks together into one studio master became more and more difficult for the engineer or producer as the tracks became more complicated.

The rotary knobs on the mixing consoles were known as *turn pots* because you turned them to alter the amount of voltage going through a potentiometer under each knob. Because these turn pots were sometimes as large as two inches in diameter, it was impossible to control more than four at once, and even then it was difficult to do if all four dials needed to move at the same time. Many times, extra studio employees were drafted into the control room to help "perform" a mix, and it often took many rehearsals and takes of the mix to get it right.

Tom Dowd, a brilliant young engineer at Atlantic Records, was responsible for recording and producing some of the finest artists of the 1960s and 1970s, including John Coltrane, Charles Mingus, Dizzy Gillespie, Ray Charles, Aretha Franklin, Otis Redding, Cream, and Lynyrd Skynyrd. Dowd had been a musician in high school, had studied physics at Columbia University, and had worked on atomic physics as part of the Manhattan Project during the Second World War. He came to Atlantic Records with a wealth of musical skill as well as physics knowledge and engineering abilities. Dowd loved to

Figure 7-5. Mixing console with rotary dials (turn pots).

record in eight tracks but realized the limitations of working with eight tracks simultaneously on a mixing console. To make things easier, he converted the rotary knobs on the console to vertical faders by replacing the turn pot mechanism with slide wire. By doing that, he discovered he could control as many as ten faders at once, each fitting conveniently under one of his ten fingers. Therefore, he could mix eight tracks at once and also control a master fader all by himself. By doing this, Tom Dowd gave rise to the modern mixing desk in which all channels are fed through vertical faders and each channel strip contains its own controls for pre-amp, inserts, sends, compression, EQ, and volume. The Mix view that you use in Studio One to mix and master your work is a direct emulation of the type of mixing desk that Tom Dowd created at Atlantic.

Figure 7-6. Rack mountable mixing desk with vertical faders.

Dowd's development of the mixing desk and the continued development of magnetic tape technology made it possible for companies to build studio mixing desks with increasing numbers of channels (32-track, 64-track, 128-track, and so on). Of course, as the number of tracks increased, the complexity of mixing returned to the days when all studio employees were brought into the studio to rehearse and perform a mix again, except that now each participant in the mix might be responsible for up to ten tracks, and it was sometimes challenging to get everybody around the desk at the same time.

In the early 1990s, Yamaha created the first digital mixers that included the ability to write and recall automation of faders and rotary dials. These new "flying faders" allowed engineers to program a mix into the console and then have the desk perform the entire mix by itself as the master studio copy was made. Modern Digital Audio Workstations all contain some degree of mixing desk emulation, and some high-end DAWs, such as Pro Tools HD, can also control the physical faders from the computer. In fact, with the advent of the Internet and networked studios, it is now possible for someone

Figure 7-7. Midas, digital live mixing console.

in New York to control the faders of a console in Los Angeles in real time, just by using a laptop computer or even an iPad.

PROJECT G: THE FINAL PRESENTATION

Your final task is to use either Keynote or PowerPoint to create a presentation of all the music you have created for your imaginary video game and relate the whole story of the game. Your presentation should include a beginning slide that announces the title of your game and your name. The next slides should tell the story of the game, with one slide per scene, level, or world in your game, and you may include scans of any graphics you have drawn for the game. Each slide should have your mixed, mastered, and exported video game music embedded so that the people who read your slides will hear the music that you have composed for the game. The final slide should thank your audience for reading your story and listening to your music and give them a sense of when you expect this new game to go into production.

HELPFUL TIPS

- When you create a Keynote or PowerPoint presentation, keep your background plain and use a readable font for your story. If your description is too large to fit onto one slide per scene, level, or world, it is better to use several slides rather than use a small font that might be unreadable.

- Export all your video game music from Studio One using the method that we learned in the Bonus Skill section in Chapter Six. If you have purchased the Studio One MP3 Export Function, it would be best to export all your mixes as MP3s so that they load and run quickly in Keynote or PowerPoint. If you are exporting as WAV format files, you can use a utility such as iTunes or http://audioformat.com/wav-to-mp3 to convert your files.

- To insert music onto a slide in Keynote, select Choose from the Insert menu and navigate to the song you wish to insert. As you insert the music, the panel on the right will allow you to specify whether the music will play automatically or when you click it. Uncheck this box so it starts automatically when the slide loads. Keynote will place a small badge on the slide that contains a play icon and a mute icon. You should move this off to the left of the slide so it does not appear when the slide loads.

- To insert music onto a slide in PowerPoint, choose Movies and Sounds from the Insert menu and navigate to the song you want to insert. Use the Custom Animation dialog to tell the program to play the song directly after the previous slide, and then move the speaker icon off the slide itself so that it will not appear during the slide show.

- When you have completed all your slides and have added all your music, you should set the times for which each slide plays.

  To do this in Keynote, use the Play > Record Show option. Click the red Record button at the bottom of the screen and go through each slide, allowing the music to play fully before moving to the next slide. Click the red Record button again to end recording at the end of your presentation. To play the timed slideshow back again, select Play > Play Recorded Show.

  To set slide times in PowerPoint, select the Slideshow > Rehearse Timings option, and the program will keep a record of the timings of each slide. After you rehearse the timings, PowerPoint will ask if you wish to keep those timings. If you are happy with the timings, select Yes.

- Check through your presentation for timings and for accuracy in your text. Nothing can derail a presentation quite like glaring spelling mistakes or grammatical errors displayed for all to read or music that launches in the wrong place or cuts off prematurely.

PROJECT REQUIREMENTS CHECKLIST

Your project should include

- Several different mixes of your video game music.
- An opening slide that introduces you and your video game.
- Individual slides for each scene, level, or world in your game.
- Different video game mixes embedded and starting automatically on each slide.
- A concluding slide thanking your audience and announcing the expected production date of your game.
- A written statement of your challenges and successes in completing this project.

NOTES AND RESOURCES FOR TEACHERS 8

THE CREATIVE PROCESS AND ASSESSMENT: AUTHOR'S PERSPECTIVE

Children are naturally inquisitive. Children are naturally creative. These two facts alone have driven my teaching strategies since I began teaching in 1990, and these facts are behind the approach taken throughout this book toward teaching composition.

As children grow, they become inhibited in their creativity. This is probably because we start to teach them about "right notes" and "wrong notes," or we begin to direct their compositional journey through the lens of 18th- and 19th-century tonal music harmony practices.

With creativity, the journey is most important, not the end product. When we teach through composition, it is vital that we value every experiment and choice that our students make so that we encourage them to continue tapping into their creative and inquisitive potentials. By continuing to experiment, children will begin to find their own musical voice and discover what is appropriate melodically, harmonically, and rhythmically. We should encourage them to take risks, to learn from their choices, and to use their own experiences to inform their further development.

The practice of composition is not about writing notes on a piece of paper and then playing them on the instrument to see what they sound like; it is about finding notes on the instrument and then learning how to write those on paper or record them so that others can hear and enjoy them.

Students should listen to a lot of music. Use the recommended examples in this chapter as well as any music that you are familiar with and enjoy. You will find much of this music on iTunes, Spotify, Apple Music, and YouTube. Encourage children to talk and write about music. I often encourage my students to explain music by writing a letter relating the experience of music to a friend who has recently lost his or her hearing (this approach usually produces more exhaustive description of music than writing for a listening test or exam). Writing about their own compositional process and choices also allows students to solidify their learning experience and inform their future direction in composition.

Improvisation is essential to the compositional process. It is a method of trial and error that allows students to learn from their successes and challenges. Allow time for students to improvise, and provide a safe environment for it, away from criticism or correction. When children are very young, they improvise a lot on instruments to find out about combinations of notes, rhythms, and dynamics. When we begin to direct their attention away from that creative play to playing a "real tune," we unfortunately direct them away from their creative journey. Small wonder then that even professional musicians and teachers can become intimidated by the idea of improvisation. Remember that the great composers themselves were improvisers. Bach was well known for his improvisational skill, as were Liszt, Paganini, Chopin, Mozart, Beethoven, Gershwin, and many others. Improvisation is not about making all students into jazz geniuses like Charlie Parker, Miles Davis, or John Coltrane—it's about letting children know that the way to create music is to make it up themselves without fear. Encourage students to experiment to find notes, rhythms, melodies, and bass lines that they like, and then record them into their compositions. Many of my own students use Musicloops as guides to improvise with and then delete or mute the Musicloops when they have recorded their own ideas.

The reproducible project sheets included in this chapter should allow you to do both formative and summative assessment on each project. Feel free to alter them as you will, depending on your own teaching style. Students' responses on the writing portion should allow both you and them to see where they are succeeding and how their process can develop as they move on through the projects. The list of required elements in each project sheet allows students to have a checklist as they compose. (I always let students keep the blank rubric in their class folder as we start each project.) The early project sheets include many more examples of concrete tasks than the later projects—these allow students to understand that as they progress through the projects, the necessary skills to use the software become a spoken-for part of their creative success. The process is not about learning the software, but about learning to be creative.

The written steps go hand in hand with the videos on the book's companion website, so use both. A child who is not good at book learning may be excellent at learning from the visual approach of the video. Similarly, a child who is not good at learning visually may benefit from the written descriptions of each step of the skills. Let your students learn in whatever way is comfortable to them, and give them time and space to compose. If students are happy that they have a safe and warm learning environment, and they have the potential to earn the points for each part of the project, they will be more likely to experiment freely with composition because they can see that the process is not about the right or wrong notes, but about the journey. The creative journey is theirs—this book shows them the path.

RECOMMENDED EXAMPLES OF ELECTRONIC MUSIC FOR LISTENING

Mike Oldfield: *Tubular Bells*

Jean-Michel Jarre: *Oxygene*

Vangelis: *Albedo 0.39*

Kraftwerk: *Autobahn*

Tangerine Dream: *Underwater Sunlight*

The Art of Noise: *(Who's Afraid of) The Art of Noise?*

Orbital: *In Sides*

Paul van Dyk: *Volume: The Best of Paul van Dyk*

Above and Beyond: *Group Therapy*

Imogen Heap: *Ellipse*

The M Machine: *Metropolis*

Depeche Mode: *Violator*

Kodomo: *Frozen In Motion*

Shpongle: *Tales of the Inexpressible*

Brian Eno and Rick Holland: *Drums Between the Bells*

Radiohead: *Kid A*

Future Sound of London: *Accelerator*

Portishead: *Dummy*

Massive Attack: *Blue Lines*

Vienna Teng: *Aims*

Deadmau5: *Five Years of Mau5*

RECOMMENDED EXAMPLES OF VIDEO GAME MUSIC

Duck Tales

Pole Position

Final Fantasy X

Mega-Man 2

Castlevania II

Ys Book I and II

Streets of Rage I–IV

Minecraft

REPRODUCIBLE PROJECT SHEET: PROJECT A

On a separate sheet, or in a Pages or Word document, write about your challenges and successes with this project. What did you enjoy working on, what did you find difficult, and what new skills did you learn?

POINTS

Your own voice introducing your radio show, recorded well.	____/10
Intro music using Musicloops.	____/10
Outro music using Musicloops.	____/10
A minimum of five tracks.	____/10
At least five Musicloops, chosen using different search terms.	____/10
No more than one minute of total project length.	____/10
Color-coded and properly titled tracks.	____/10
A written summary of your challenges and successes in completing this project.	____/30
Total	_____/100

TEACHER COMMENTS

REPRODUCIBLE PROJECT SHEET: PROJECT B

On a separate sheet, or in a Pages or Word document, write about your challenges and successes with this project. What did you enjoy working on, what did you find difficult, and what new skills did you learn?

POINTS

Playford tune, transcribed accurately, with title and composer.	____/10
Three additional treble clef pitched instruments.	____/10
Instruments chosen several instrument families (guitar, brass, strings, woodwind).	____/10
Additional bass clef instrument with melody transposed correctly.	____/10
Additional instrument transposed a fourth below the melody.	____/10
Drum part with drum patterns chosen from Drum Library.	____/10
Music mixed panned appropriately in Virtual Mixer.	____/10
A written summary of your challenges and successes in completing this project.	____/30
Total	_____/100

TEACHER COMMENTS

REPRODUCIBLE PROJECT SHEET: PROJECT C

On a separate sheet, or in a Pages or Word document, write about your challenges and successes with this project. What did you enjoy working on, what did you find difficult, and what new skills did you learn?

POINTS

Beat A, properly recorded, quantized and humanized.	____/10
Beat B, properly recorded, quantized and humanized.	____/10
Beat C, properly recorded, quantized and humanized.	____/10
Beats arranged in ABACA order.	____/10
Tracks properly labeled and color-coded.	____/10
Beats well mixed and panned appropriately.	____/10
Effective use of compression and EQ in mixing.	____/10
A written summary of your challenges and successes in completing this project.	____/30
Total	_____/100

TEACHER COMMENTS

REPRODUCIBLE PROJECT SHEET: PROJECT D

On a separate sheet, or in a Pages or Word document, write about your challenges and successes with this project. What did you enjoy working on, what did you find difficult, and what new skills did you learn?

POINTS

Eight measure chord sequence, using only diatonic chords.	____/10
No less than four repetitions of the chord sequence.	____/10
Final chord of C major.	____/10
Bass line moving in contrary motion to treble voice.	____/10
Combinations of block chords and broken chords.	____/10
Melody played on at least one instrument.	____/10
Appropriate use of tempo and dynamic markings.	____/10
A written summary of your challenges and successes in completing this project.	____/30
Total	_____/100

TEACHER COMMENTS

REPRODUCIBLE PROJECT SHEET: PROJECT E

On a separate sheet, or in a Pages or Word document, write about your challenges and successes with this project. What did you enjoy working on, what did you find difficult, and what new skills did you learn?

POINTS

A section of at least 8 measures.	____/20
B section of at least 8 measures.	____/20
Final section that returns to the original A section, with decoration and embellishment.	____/20
At least three different Virtual Instruments used in the music.	____/10
A written summary of your challenges and successes in completing this project.	____/30
Total	_____/100

TEACHER COMMENTS

REPRODUCIBLE PROJECT SHEET: PROJECT F

On a separate sheet, or in a Pages or Word document, write about your challenges and successes with this project. What did you enjoy working on, what did you find difficult, and what new skills did you learn?

POINTS

60–90 measures of music.	____/10
4-measure motifs that repeat three times, for a total of 16 measures.	____/10
Subtle fading at the end of each motif.	____/10
Accurate and appropriate quantizing and editing.	____/10
A written explanation of your basic ideas for the video game.	____/30
A written summary of your challenges and successes in completing this project.	____/30
Total	____/100

TEACHER COMMENTS

REPRODUCIBLE PROJECT SHEET: PROJECT G

On a separate sheet, or in a Pages or Word document, write about your challenges and successes with this project. What did you enjoy working on, what did you find difficult, and what new skills did you learn?

POINTS

Several different mixes of your video game music.	____/10
An opening slide that introduces you and your video game.	____/10
Individual slides describing each scene, level or world in your game.	____/30
Different video game mixes embedded and starting automatically on each slide.	____/10
A concluding slide thanking your audience and announcing the expected production date of your game.	____/10
A written statement of your challenges and success in completing this project.	____/30
Total	_____/100

TEACHER COMMENTS

INDEX

acoustics, 15
Ampex, 101–103
Atlantic Records, 114
audio interface, 2–7, 9, 16, 23, 50,
        93
    PreSonus Audiobox USB, 7, 11,
        14, 39, 89
automation, 1, 14 69, 74–75, 80,
        91, 105–106, 109, 116
bass line, 57–59, 68, 71, 78–80,
        87–88, 95, 122, 128
beat boxing, 39
Berliner, Emile, 16, 89, 99, 100
breakpoints, 15
bus, 14, 39, 48–49, 113
chords, 11, 21, 27, 39, 55–60,
        62–63, 67–68, 71, 78–83, 88,
        91, 95, 128
    block chords, 55, 58, 67–68, 128
    broken chords, 55, 59, 67–68,
        128
    chord sequence, 55–60, 67–68,
        80–81, 87, 128
    chord inversion, 55, 57
clipping, 14, 90, 94, 112
composing, x, 3, 33, 39, 53, 55, 57,
        67, 69, 80, 83, 87–88, 95,
        97, 103
compression (audio effect), 39, 54,
        105, 109–110, 115, 127
computer, xi, 1–5, 8, 12–15, 19,
        22–24, 29–30, 37, 42–44, 46,
        50–52, 61–62, 64, 69, 79,
        83, 89, 93, 96, 116–117
creativity, ix–x, 121
Digital Audio Workstation (DAW)
        software, 2–3, 70, 93, 116
Dowd, Tom, 105, 114–116
drum beat, 40, 44–48, 50, 53, 64

drum fill, 40
drum notation, 31, 33
dynamics, 46, 61–64, 68, 106, 122,
        128
Edison, Thomas, 16, 89, 99
electronic music, 69–70, 79–80, 82,
        87–88, 103, 109, 123
ensemble, 21, 24, 61
EQ (audio effect), 39, 46, 48–50, 54,
        92, 105–106, 108–115, 127
fades, 1, 14–15, 72, 112
Ford, Mary, 102–103
form, 69, 78, 80, 82–83, 87–88
    binary, 69, 78, 80, 82, 87
    bridge, 71
    chorus, 55
    extended ternary, 88
    rondo, 88
    ternary, 69, 83, 87–88
    verse, 55
Gibson, 103
Gramophone, 99–100
guitar fretboard, 23
Hal Leonard, 23, 66–67
harmony, 31, 35, 55–56, 68, 78–79,
        121, 128
    diatonic harmony, 55–56, 68,
        78–79, 128
headphones, 3–5, 7–8, 11, 14, 16,
        28, 48, 50–51, 58, 71, 90,
        106, 111
hearing, 3, 8, 15, 35, 51–52, 86,
        110, 122
Hughes, David Edward, 1, 16–17
humanize, 39, 44–45, 54, 80, 127
improvisation, x, 79, 122
Jobs, Steve, ix
"kick-snare-kick-snare" pattern,
        39–41, 43–44, 48

latency, 39, 50–52

loops, x, 1, 10–15, 18–19, 39, 50, 64, 79, 88, 110, 122, 125

lyrics, 39, 61–62, 65

making beats, 39, 41

mastering, 105, 110–113

melody, 21, 24, 27, 29, 31, 35, 37, 39, 55, 57, 60–63, 67–68, 80–82, 126, 128

metronome (click), 12, 28, 43–44, 60, 80, 90–91, 96

microphone, 1–8, 10, 15–18, 29, 45, 51, 90, 93, 95, 99, 113
  carbon microphone, 16
  condenser microphone, 3, 6–7, 17–18, 95
  dynamic microphone, 6, 17
  phantom power, 6–7, 90, 94–95
  PreSonus M7 microphone, 1, 18, 95
  ribbon microphone, 6, 17

MIDI Controller, 3, 4, 21, 23, 27–28, 39, 42, 50, 52, 56, 58, 70–74, 83, 89
  PreSonus PS-49 MIDI Controller, 4, 21, 23, 39, 70, 74, 83, 89

mixer, 7–9, 11, 19, 23, 32, 35, 37, 39, 46–49, 51, 90, 93, 111, 116, 126

mixing, 6, 14, 36–37, 45–46, 50, 105–106, 109–110, 112–117, 127

mixdown, 98–99

motif, x, 89, 95–97, 103–104, 107

Moog, Robert, 69, 86–87

MP3, 65, 98, 111–112, 118

music printing, 22, 55, 65, 69
  Petrucci method, 65
  printing press, 22, 65
  Rastell method, 65–66

music theory, x, 22–23, 79
  beat, 12, 22, 28, 40, 44, 45, 54, 61, 91, 96, 127
  key, x, 22, 56, 60, 66, 78, 83
  key signature, 2, 22, 25–26, 29
  major, 25, 33, 56–57, 68, 78–79, 83, 128
  measure, x, 22, 25–29, 31, 40, 43, 45–46, 48, 50, 53–54,

56–62, 68, 80–82, 88, 95–97, 104, 128–129
  minor, 56, 78–79, 83
  rhythm, 3, 22, 31, 39–40, 44, 51, 79, 82, 87, 95, 121–122
  scale, 21–22, 56–57, 60
  staff, 22–23, 25–26, 28, 30–31, 56, 58–60, 63, 65–66
  time signature, 2, 22, 25, 29

National Core Arts Standards (NCAS), ix

Nimbit, 64, 99

notation, 2, 21–24, 30–33, 37, 40, 70, 97

notation software, 2–4, 15, 23, 61, 69

Notion, xi, 4–5, 15, 21, 23–33, 35, 37, 39, 51–53, 55, 58–64, 68–70, 97
  Audio tab, 23, 53
  entry palette, 25–28, 58–59, 62–63
  Score Setup screen, 25, 29, 31, 36, 59–60
  virtual keyboard, 27, 31, 58–59
  virtual mixer, 32, 25, 37, 126

online companion, 2, 5, 75

overdubbing, 99, 102–103

Pachelbel, Johann, 57

panning (audio effect), 14, 34, 46, 50, 86, 106–109
  phantom center, 33–34
  stereo, 33, 35

panorama effect, 33

Paul, Les, 89, 101–103, 114

Pfluemer, Fritz, 89, 100

phonograph, 99–100

piano keyboard, 23, 27, 43, 58, 71, 78, 86

Playford, John, 21, 24–25, 29, 31, 35–36, 66, 126

preset, 41, 45–50, 53, 69–71, 73–75, 80–81, 92, 96, 106, 108, 111–112

PreSonus Music Creation Suite, 1, 3–6, 18, 70, 89, 93, 99, 111

quantize, 39, 44–45, 54, 80–81, 103, 127

recording, 1–3, 6, 8–11, 15–16, 18–19, 21–22, 24, 28, 33,

35, 37, 39, 41, 45, 51–52, 60, 66, 68, 73, 75, 89–103, 110, 114, 118

recording tape, 9, 100–101
    cassette tape, 9
    pre-roll and post-roll, 9
    reel-to-reel tape, 9, 101
Rockmore, Clara, 85
score, 25–32, 36–37, 55, 58–63, 65, 68
    full score, 32, 61
    lead sheet, 21
    parts, 23, 29, 32, 37, 55, 61–64
send, 49, 93, 113–115
sequencing, 1, 10
sheet music, 22, 24, 55, 65–67
soft synth, 69–70, 72, 74, 78–80, 82, 87, 89, 96
sound on sound recording, 102, 114
speakers (monitors), 3, 16, 33, 50–51, 111, 113
STEAM (Science, Technology, Engineering, Arts, Math), ix, 5, 15, 33, 50, 65, 83, 99, 114
STEAM Problem Solving, 5, 15, 33, 50, 65, 83, 99, 114
stomps, 94
Studio One, x–xi, 1, 4–6, 8–16, 23, 27, 32, 37, 39, 41–45, 48–54, 64–65, 69–70, 73–75, 78–80, 83, 87–98, 105, 107–108, 110–113, 115, 118
    Ampire, 89, 94
    Arrange view, 11–15, 39, 41, 45, 48, 54, 64, 70, 74–75, 79–82, 91, 96, 98, 106–107
    audio event, 8–9, 12–13
    Audio Setup screen, 11, 52
    browser, 11–13, 15, 41, 45, 49–50, 70–71, 74–75, 80, 92, 94, 96, 106, 112
    Channel Strip Effect, 92, 105, 110
    Compressor Effect, 49–50, 92, 105–112, 114
    Edit view, 9, 12–13, 80
    editing tools, 89, 91

Impact, 39, 41–47, 49–50, 53–54, 69–71, 75, 78, 82–83, 88, 96, 110
instrument data event, 13
instrument editor, 43–44, 46
Limiter effect, 92, 105, 112
Mai Tai, 69–71, 75–76, 78, 81, 87–88
Mix view, 13–15, 32, 46, 54, 92, 106, 109, 111, 114–115
Mojito, 69–75, 78, 81–82, 87–88
Musicloops, 1, 10–15, 18–19, 39, 50, 64, 79, 88, 110, 122, 125
Presence, 69–72, 74–75, 77–78, 80–81, 87–88
Pro EQ effect, 49, 92, 106, 108–109, 111–112, 114
Sample One, 69–71, 75, 77–78, 88
track, 6–10, 12–15, 18–19, 39, 41, 43–46, 48–50, 53–54, 70, 73–74, 78–83, 89–90, 92–95, 105–114, 125, 127
sub-mix, 48
swing, 21, 32, 35
synthesizer (synth), 69–75, 78–83, 86–87, 89, 96
    amp, 69, 71–72, 74–75, 87
    envelope (ADSR), 69, 72–74, 87
    filter, 69, 71–75, 80
        cutoff, 72–74
        resonance, 73–74
    low-frequency oscillator (LFO), 72–73, 86
    modulation, 73, 112
    monophonic, 71, 82
    oscillator, 69, 71–72, 75, 86
    portamento, 71–72
tablature, 21–22, 30, 33
tempo (bpm), 11–13, 28, 43, 45, 60–62, 64, 68, 90, 96–97, 128
Theremin (electronic instrument), 85–86
Theremin, Léon, 69, 84–86
transducer, 16
transport, 8–9, 12, 15, 27–28, 43, 48, 60, 73, 80, 90, 96

cycle region, 48, 73
Play, 11, 27, 43, 48, 60, 74, 90,
    96, 100
Return-to-Zero, 27, 44, 90
Stop, 8, 11–12, 28, 43, 48, 73,
    80, 90
transpose, 30–31, 37, 69, 83, 126
vibration, 15–16, 18, 99
virtual instrument, 42, 69–70,
    74–75, 78, 81–82, 88–89,
    92, 110, 129

voltage, 15–18, 86, 114
volume, 1, 10–11, 14–15, 35,
    46–48, 50, 63, 72, 74, 81,
    84, 86, 91, 106–107, 109,
    111–115
WAV format, 11, 37, 64–65, 67, 98,
    118
waveform, 8–9, 13, 15–16
    amplitude, 84, 86
    frequency, 84, 86
Yamaha, 116